ROLES OF MAN

DATE DUE			
Mar 29'73			
Apr 12'73			

ROLES OF MAN

An Introduction to the Social Sciences

DEENA AND MICHAEL WEINSTEIN

The Dryden Press Inc.
Hinsdale, Illinois

To our Parents who, when we said,
"Everybody does it,"
responded,
"You're not everybody."

PREFACE

There is only one human condition, but there are many sciences for studying it. This paradox has been the source of intellectual unrest for social scientists concerned with unifying the study of man and for teachers and students involved in courses introducing the social sciences.

In general, there are three ways of attempting to resolve the paradox. First, one can be eclectic and combine in a haphazard way concepts and data from the various social sciences. On completion of such an effort one will be left with some understanding of the different social sciences, but will have little or no unified knowledge of the human condition. Second, one can say that a particular social science is the most important one, and that the entire human condition can be illuminated in its terms. In this case one will attain a coherent vision of the human condition, but will fail to appreciate the special perspectives of each social science. Thus, the first two attempts to resolve the paradox lead to the conclusion that to maximize unified knowledge of the human condition is to minimize understanding of the different social sciences, and *vice versa*.

One should not jump to conclusions. There is a third way of resolving the paradox in which one tries to find, behind the apparent variety of the social sciences, a common thread of understanding. If such an attempt succeeds, the unity of the human condition appears within the diversity of the social sciences.

This book is an attempt to resolve the paradox in the third way. We try to show throughout the following pages that the concept of role can unify understanding of the different social sciences and thereby unify understanding of the human condition. If our effort succeeds, a person who reads this book will carry away with him not only isolated facts and concepts about culture, human relations, and personal choice, but also some insight into what it means to be human.

The basic theme of the book is the debate between the social self ("me") which represents roles, and the individual self ("I") which represents creative choice. The terms I and me are taken from the philosophy of George Herbert Mead, the twentieth-century American pragmatist, who devoted much of his professional career to showing that the nature of the human self is dialogic. The notion that human existence is an ongoing debate clarified by the various social sciences is the idea that unifies what appears in the following pages.

The book begins with a discussion of how the human self develops from infancy to adulthood. The second and third chapters explore the way the concept of role is used by anthropologists and students of cultural conflict. In these chapters role is defined as a recipe for human action. The fourth chapter investigates the use of role by students of social organization. Here and in the following four chapters role is defined as the actual expectations of behavior in social situations. The following four chapters explore the use of role in the disciplines of economics, political science, learning and communication, and sociology. The ninth chapter explores that part of social psychology which investigates the ways in which role behaviors are mediated through such relations as competition, cooperation, conflict, and concord. The tenth chapter discusses those parts of social psychology and psychology which seek to describe the ways in which roles are integrated into human personalities. Finally, the eleventh chapter explores the ways in which human freedom is realized in the debate between "I" and "me."

This book is intended primarily for use in courses introducing the social sciences. It is meant to provide the continuity of analysis that is so often sought by those who teach and take such courses. It is also meant to provide a humanistic perspective on the social sciences which will make these studies more meaningful and exciting to all concerned. Aside from its primary use, the book is also well adapted for introductory courses to any of the particular social sciences. In such courses it will provide students with a way of viewing the major relations between the social science he is primarily studying and the other social sciences.

We hope that this book provides a unified and coherent perspective on the social sciences and the human condition. We have attempted to avoid narrow approaches without sacrificing consistency and continuity. We believe that knowledge of the social sciences provides insights into important concrete situations in human existence, and have tried to show that this is so in the following pages.

We would like to thank Mr. Joseph Byers, our editor at the Dryden Press, for his understanding and aid in this project. We would also like to thank our students, who never fail to broaden and deepen our appreciation of social life.

West Lafayette, Spring, 1971

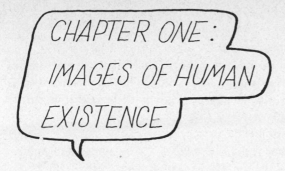

CHAPTER ONE:
IMAGES OF HUMAN
EXISTENCE

The *social sciences* are basically organized ways of thinking about the objects, relations, and hopes of human beings. In the natural sciences, investigators study the physical and organic world in which human beings exist, by suggesting relations among events and testing to see whether these relations occur. In the social sciences, investigators perform the same activities of proposing and testing, but their subject is the process of human existence.

THE IMAGE OF HUMAN EXISTENCE IN EVERYDAY LIFE

One of the several characteristics that distinguish human beings from the rest of the world is their thinking about themselves. Human beings make their desires, relations, and activities objects of study.

Every human being who participates in worthwhile relations with others has a set of principles about the objects, relations, and hopes of men. When a certain set of principles is widely held in a group of people it is called *common sense*.

The common-sense view of human existence varies according to time and place. The common-sense view is not the only way of looking at human life. Each of the great religions of the world has a view of human life. In this book we will discuss the view of social scientists. In the Middle Ages the common-sense view was that human beings had immortal souls and were placed on earth as a preparation for a final judgment about whether they would go to heaven or hell. For the medieval man social arrangements existed to aid the salvation of souls and to control the effects of sinful actions. Many people in the Middle Ages believed that society included angels, demons, and other spirits, and they devised elaborate practices to encourage these spirits to aid them in the realization of their plans. Someone who questioned the existence of such demons would be greeted by shock and hostility. If a medieval man did not take precautions against the spirit world, his fellow human beings would regard him as highly impractical. While parts of the medieval common-sense view persist in today's Western world, much of this perspective has been replaced by other notions.

The common-sense view of human existence that is most widespread in the contemporary Western world has been described by the American political scientist Arthur F. Bentley. Bentley investigated the principles about the objects, relations, and hopes of men that appear in everyday speech. He found that for "most of us all of the time, for all of us most of the time, it is quite sufficient to regard human beings as 'persons' who possess qualities or motives which are phases of their character and who act in accordance with these qualities or this character, under certain conditions of life in which they are placed."[1] When someone does a kindly act, we say that he did it because he was good-natured. When someone tries to take advantage of another person we remark bitterly that it is another example of human nature. We say that people behave heroically because they are brave and that others shrink in fear because they are cowards.

The method of stating that certain actions are performed because individuals have certain qualities embedded in their natures is frequently extended to account for the behavior of entire groups. We say that the United States has an advanced industrial technology because Americans have ingenuity and that the production of some goods in Germany is efficient because the Germans have a passion for order. Taken to an extreme, this pattern of thought leads to the idea that human groups have minds of their own. Some people talk about nations choosing to go to war or deciding to adopt a particular religious faith. The most widespread common-sense view of human existence in the contemporary Western world conceives of individuals and groups as things ruled by characteristic natures.

CRITICISM OF EVERYDAY SPEECH

People who study the social sciences do not leave their common-sense conceptions at the library door. They assume that social scientists discuss human existence in terms of individuals with a human nature, groups with definable interests and nations with discernible purposes. This assumption often leads them to misunderstand the social sciences. In general, social scientists do not adopt the common-sense view of human existence because they find that it contains many significant problems. The long-range views or perspectives of human existence devised by social scientists provide new and fresh ways of interpreting the life of man. These perspectives of human existence are the most important contributions that social scientists have made to civilization, and they can be understood by all literate people. The perspectives of the social sciences are attempts to overcome the problems that appear in the common-sense view of human existence.

Social scientists criticize the common-sense view of human existence because it confuses words and things. In the common-sense view of human existence people mistake words for things by accepting a word describing a meaningful human activity as evidence of a thing causing that activity. For example, when we see someone behave heroically, we say that he is a brave man. What does this mean? It can mean that the term brave man is a convenient way of describing a person who performs heroic actions. In this case a brave man is someone whom we observe performing brave actions. The phrase can also mean that we believe that a thing called bravery caused the performance of heroic actions. Most social scientists hold that this use of everyday speech is misleading. How does one know that a person is brave apart from his performing heroic actions? How would one identify and observe the thing called bravery? Most social scientists believe that one cannot know that a person is brave apart from his actions, and that there is no thing called bravery. Thus the common-sense view of human existence leads one to confuse words and things; words such as bravery, which are used correctly to describe processes and actions, are misused to refer to nonexistent things or objects.

The mistake of confusing words and things occurs throughout the common-sense view of human existence. The most serious instances of this mistake occur in notions of human nature and group character. In general, people hold that a force called *human nature* is responsible for the activity of individuals. Some people believe that human nature is good, others that it is corrupt, and others that it is split between good and evil. In each case the only way that the person can test his conception of human nature is by observing the activities of men and women. Many social scientists conclude that since human nature can only be known through the observation of behavior, it is not necessary to use the concept of human nature at all. The same case applies to notions of group and national character: the character of a nation or a group is revealed in the pattern of its activities.

There are other reasons to question the common-sense view of human existence. Using the example of human nature, it is possible to show that the method of common sense is either meaningless or false. The person who claims that human nature is good is faced with the problem of accounting for evil actions. If he states that underneath his evil actions man is inherently good, he is making a declaration of faith rather than a statement of fact. If he states that man is good but his society is bad, he must explain human beings not being found outside of relations with one another. If he states that man can be brought to lead the good life, he has admitted that man is not completely good now. If he states that what appears to be evil is really good in some wider context that we cannot fully understand, he has evaded the problem. The person who claims that human nature is evil is in no better position. He must account for the occurrence of good actions. The person who claims that human nature is split between good and evil appears to have a stronger case. However, his argument turns out to be meaningless because he is only saying that sometimes people behave well and sometimes badly.

Social scientists in the twentieth century have surpassed the common-sense view of human existence by defining the concepts of social role and social self. These concepts avoid the mistake of confusing words and things.

HUMAN EXISTENCE AND SOCIAL ROLE

Some uses of ordinary language indicate views of human existence different from the perspective of common sense. Often human beings pose such questions as, "What will people think if I do this?" or "What should one do in this situation?" The words people and one in these questions point to a dimension of human existence that human beings do not ordinarily consider as separate in their everyday lives. The study of the dimension of human existence revealed by the words people and one is the basis of inquiry in the social sciences.

The question, "What will people think if I do this?," assumes that the person who asks it can think about his own actions. Human beings can think about themselves, and study their desires, relations, and activities from various points of view.

The ability of human beings to think about themselves was emphasized by the philosopher and social psychologist, George Herbert Mead. Mead held that the human self is made up of two parts, the "I" and the "me." The *"me"* is "a system of attitudes which the self cherishes and which it has acquired in communication with other members of the community, both living and dead."[2] The "me" is the social component of the self, because it is mainly a product of learning from others. The infant does not come into the world with ideas about human existence. Judgments about what is good, true, and right are gradually learned through childhood. Yet the individual makes a contribution to human existence. The *"I"* or individual component of the self thinks of futures different from the present and attempts to bring them into existence. Human existence can be seen as an interplay between the social "me" and the creative "I." For example, the "I" may suggest participation in a civil rights demonstration. The "me" may respond with statements that parents, future employers, and fraternity brothers disapprove of people who demonstrate. Eventually the person will resolve this debate by joining the demonstration or staying away. When people talk to themselves about a plan of action, there is a conversation between "I" and "me." The "I" proposes, the "me" criticizes, the whole person acts.

The *self* is a conversation between "me" and "I." Human beings are neither empty bottles into which social content is poured nor self-sufficient creators. Without social and individual parts of the self the key experience of planning would not be possible. The fact that a person can think about himself "makes it possible for him to evaluate and criticize his self and to compare his own self with the selves of others and with an improved self which he hopes to achieve through personal effort."[3] The "me" provides the materials from which the "I" creates an individual existence. Without a language learned from others and the ability to predict what others will do, people could neither form plans nor carry them out. Mead's idea of the self contains two fundamental truths about human beings. First, human beings do not create something out of nothing. They are able to choose among alternatives only after they have learned about their possibilities in social relations.

People learn about their possibilities by watching others and listening to them. Second, human beings do not quietly accept traditions. They change their existence by creating images of the future and by acting to put these images into being. People make new possibilities for others by putting their own dreams into existence for others to see.

There are great advantages to studying the conversation between "I" and "me" rather than either one separately. The student who forgets the "I" and concentrates only on the "me" will tend to think of people as robots who mechanically act out the deeds required by the rules they have learned. He will think of human beings as talking animals, completely determined by forces outside of them. The student who forgets the "me" and concentrates only on the "I" will tend to think of people as free spirits, capable of putting their wildest dreams into action. At an extreme he will believe as long as people wish hard enough they will get what they want.

Human beings are neither talking animals nor free spirits. They are continuously engaged in a conversation within themselves. Students who concentrate only on the "me" cannot account for the novelty that keeps appearing in human life. Students who concentrate only on the "I" cannot account for the high predictability of most human action. This is why the best social scientists think about human life and human relations in terms of conversation and debate. This is why the conversation between "I" and "me" is the basis of this book.

While not ignoring the "I," social scientists have been primarily concerned with studying the "me." When an individual asks the question, "What will people think if I do this?," he will look for the answer in the attitudes and judgments that compose the "me." His question really means, "What is a person expected by others to do in this situation?" For example, a new recruit in the army might wonder about the differences between military and civilian life. The individual does not ordinarily answer his questions by asking others what they expect him to do, although he does do this sometimes. The recruit might ask his sergeant to fill him in on army life. Further, the person does not usually try to imagine what some particular other person expects him to do, although he also does this sometimes. The recruit might imagine what a friend of his, who had been in the army, would do. In general, the person answers the question by discovering a rule for acting in the situation that forms a part of the "me." The recruit might remember the rule, "Obey your superior, and wait for his orders." Throughout his life, a person learns rules of expected action that apply in different situations. Some of these rules cluster together and define expected actions related to the performance of a

THE HUMAN SELF

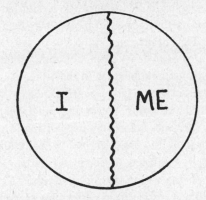

PRINCIPLE:
SOCIAL SCIENTISTS STUDY
THE INTERPLAY BETWEEN
"I" AND "ME"

"I"	"ME"
1. PROPOSES NEW PLANS	1. CRITICIZES PLANS
2. THINKS BEYOND SOCIAL ROLES	2. REPRESENTS SOCIAL ROLES
3. CREATES	3. PRESERVES
4. ORIGINATES	4. CONFORMS
5. INVENTS	5. ADAPTS

task. For example, the rules of handling a car in traffic define the task of driving. Such clusters of rules are called *roles*. Associated with the task of curing illnesses are the roles of doctor, nurse, patient, hospital administrator, insurance investigator, and medical supply salesman. There are many other roles associated with just this task.

LEARNING SOCIAL ROLES

Socialization, the process of learning social roles, occurs in several stages. As an infant the human being is aware of neither physical nor social limitations. The infant is not in an enviable position. When the mature human being experiences a desire he can often take measures to satisfy it, or substitute another desire for it that can be satisfied. For example, someone who is trying to stop smoking may substitute the desire for candy for the desire for a cigarette. If the mature human being experiences frustration in the pursuit of gratification, he can frequently delay his impulsive behavior and try to find efficient ways of attaining satisfaction. For example, a man who would like to gain the attention of a woman may delay his impulse to meet her immediately and devise a plan to impress her. The infant can neither act to satisfy desires nor think of ways to obtain gratification. He is dependent upon others for gratification and does not know how to communicate with the others.

The child gains self-awareness through learning a language. He is taught to express his desires through making requests in words. Words are sounds that have meanings. They refer to objects, experiences, and actions, and they are understood by a group of human beings. As the child learns to express his desires in words, he also learns that he is expected to act in certain ways depending upon the situation. Along with the ability to call upon others for specific aid come requirements to perform or refrain from performing certain actions. Along with rights come duties.

At first the child experiences the regulations as external impositions. He does not see the situation from any perspective but his own and follows the rules mechanically. After a time, the "me" develops to the point that the child can see the situation from the perspective of particular others, like his mother or his father. He is able to realize that his mother and father will be angry if he ruins household furniture. He learns that one part of the role of child is to refrain from ruining property. At this point, the child is incapable of asking, "What will people think if I do this?" He can only ask such questions as, "What will my mother think if I do this?" The world still revolves around him, and all social relations are relations to him.

The next stage in socialization—a social process during which an individual learns what is expected of a human being in various situations—occurs when the child learns that all people in certain categories, like child, parent, and teacher, are expected to follow certain rules. He learns that all children are expected to refrain from ruining property, and that all parents (not only his parents) are expected to protect their children. Here, the child cannot yet ask the question, "What will people think if I do this?" He can ask, "What would a parent think if I did this?" or "What should a child do in this situation?" When a child learns that all people in certain categories are expected to follow certain rules, he has understood the meaning of social role, even if he does not know the term. He has been able to go beyond his particular relations and to judge his proposed actions from a general point of view. He is able, for example, to understand the rights and duties of all parents, not only his parents. He is also able to judge what his parents do according to the standard of what all parents are supposed to do.

STAGES OF SOCIALIZATION

STAGE ONE

I

THE INFANT HAS NO "ME"

STAGE TWO

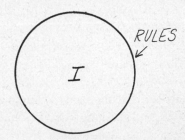

I

RULES

ALL SOCIAL RULE ARE
EXTERNALLY IMPOSED

STAGE THREE

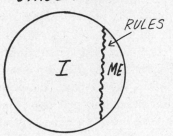

I ME

RULES

THE CHILD CAN TAKE THE ROLE
OF PARTICULAR OTHERS
(E.G. HIS PARENTS)

STAGE FOUR

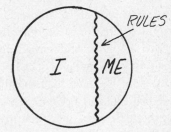

I ME

RULES

THE CHILD CAN TAKE THE
ROLE OF OTHERS IN CATEGORIES
(E.G. ANY PARENTS)

STAGE FIVE

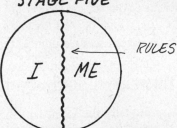

I ME

RULES

THE CHILD CAN TAKE THE ROLE OF
HUMAN BEING (E.G. A PERSON)

It is a short step from understanding social role to asking, "What will people think if I do this?" As the child grows older he learns that there are expectations for the behavior of human beings apart from any particular role. It is possible to say that every human group has a role of human being apart from specialized roles. This role defines the behavior expected of any person in the group. The role of human being constitutes the morality of the group, and enables the person to ask, "What will people think if I do this?" Mead called the role of human being the *generalized other*.

The process of socialization follows the steps of (1) learning regulations as external impositions, (2) learning to take the perspective of another particular person, (3) learning to take the role of a person performing a particular task in a social action, and (4) learning to take the role of a human being in any social action. Human development, however, does not end with the completion of the socialization process. Sociologist Arnold Green notes that the "mature self not only regards itself as others view it but it also appraises others as it appraises itself."[4] Ultimately, the human being has the possibility of self-rule, of autonomy. The person can make rules for himself, and present those rules for the consideration of his fellow human beings. The creative possibility of making a rule for oneself should not be confused with the impulsive behavior of the infant. The infant knows no rules and is a slave of organic impulses and environmental conditions. The autonomous human being fully understands social roles and can surpass them by creating new rules when he finds their creation desirable. For example, the people who urge that industry become responsible for cleaning up pollution are attempting to create new rules. The mature human being is a role-player who performs social tasks, a role-taker who adopts the perspectives of others, and a role-maker who creates new rules to guide goal-seeking. The complete human being is an organism with biological impulses, a social self ("me") incorporating social roles, and a creative individual ("I") capable of making new rules for human communities. The social sciences are chiefly concerned with the social self, but often must consider the organism, environment, and creative individual. Thus, the social sciences are united in the study of social roles.

ROLE IN THE DIFFERENT SOCIAL SCIENCES

While the social sciences study the social self, they do not all investigate the same aspects of that self. The *social self* ("me") can be divided into two parts. The "me" is composed of social processes and cultural objects, such as words. *Social processes*, ways of using cultural objects in human relations, have already been mentioned with reference to learning social roles. Socialization is a social process in which the person learns what is expected of a human being in various situations. It is one part of the general process of learning called education. However, the idea of social process is incomplete. With respect to socialization, it is always possible to ask, "What is being learned?" People do not learn socialization; they engage in the process of socialization. What is learned is *culture*, or the group heritage of technologies (tools), principles of human relation (roles) and ideas. The anthropologist A. L. Kroeber has written that "the mass of learned and transmitted motor reactions, habits, techniques, ideas, and values—and the behavior they induce—is what constitutes culture."[5] While this definition seems to include social processes (behavior) as well as cultural objects, Kroeber clarifies his definition by emphasizing that culture is a human product: "Culture . . . is always first of all the *product* of men in groups: a set of ideas, attitudes, and habits—'rules' if one will—evolved by men to help them in their conduct of life."[6] Thus, the social self is a participant in social processes and a user of cultural objects.

Among other things, *anthropology* studies the various kinds of cultural objects and their development. Among these cultural objects are roles viewed as rules for acting in various situations that have been defined and are known by human beings. The anthropologist sees *roles* as sets of rights and duties relating to the performance of a function in accomplishing a task. For example, a nurse has the right to ask for cooperation from a patient, and the duty to follow the doctor's orders. *Rights* are claims on other role performers for means and actions necessary for accomplishing a task, and *duties* are obligations to give other role performers means and actions so that they can perform their functions effectively. The nurse claims cooperative action from the patient and is obliged to aid the doctor in performing his function.

The anthropologist's use of role can be illustrated by an example from the process of traditional college education. The educational process is centered around the two roles of teacher and student. The professor has the right to decide the course materials, the number of examinations that will be given, the form of the examinations, and the system of grading. He has the obligation to tell the truth and to grade students according to their performance rather than his impression of their personalities. The student has the right to learn a certain body of material and to be judged fairly on his competence. He has the obligation to refrain from interference in the process of teaching and learning by such activities as disrupting classes.

These rights and duties are well known by most professors and students in the United States. Although they are parts of roles (rules) that have been made to form the process of college education, they are not the only roles that could pattern college education. Even in the United States and Western Europe, where these roles were made, they are broken frequently. First, some professors and students merely break the rules. There are a few cases in which professors intentionally deceive students about the subject matter of their courses and some cases in which professors grade on other standards than achievement. Similarly, some students interfere with the continuance of the educational process. Second, some professors and students attempt to create alternative role definitions. There have been experiments in which professors and students jointly decided the curriculum, students graded themselves, grades were abolished altogether, and examinations were jointly made. These experiments were not merely deviations from existing rules, but attempts to create new rules. Thus, culture can be viewed as the arena for debate over role definitions.

The anthropologist views roles as definitions of rights and duties that apply in particular situations and are understood by those in the situations, but which may or may not be fulfilled in practice. Roles are recipes for accomplishing certain tasks that are available for use by people. Anthropologist Clifford Geertz has expressed this outlook on role in his definition of culture. Geertz holds that " . . . culture is best seen not as complexes of concrete behavior patterns—customs, usages, traditions, habit clusters . . . , but as a set of control mechanisms—plans, recipes, rules, instructions (what computer engineers call 'programs')—for the governing of behavior."[7] Just as there are several ways of getting from one city to another (air, water, rail, and highway), there are several ways of learning about the social sciences (large lecture, small group discussion, large lecture with weekly discussion section, teaching machine, correspondence course, independent study, personal tutorial). Each way of learning about the social sciences involves different roles. In the United States, where the human condition is complex and specialized, there are competing role definitions for most important situations. Culture is an arena for debate, not an oppressive domination.

For the purposes of this book, anthropology will be considered as the study of culture, the analysis and description of cultural objects and their development. Sociology, political science, economics, and education are studies of the major social processes. Social processes are the ways in which cultural objects can be used in human relations. Cultural objects can be related to human activity in four different ways. First, one can create, preserve, or destroy cultural objects; a house can be built, maintained in good condition, or torn down. The production and distribution of cultural objects is studied by economists. Thus, economists focus their attention on business, commercial and labor organizations, in which economic processes occur. They study how resources are assigned to the production and distribution of cultural objects. Second, one can learn how to use and create cultural objects; a person can learn to build a house. The learning process is discussed by students of education who focus their attention on the schools, the communications media, and the family. Third, one can decide how much time, space and resources will be spent on using and creating different cultural objects; local officials decide what kind of structures can be built in different areas (zoning laws). The process of making authoritative policies is studied by political scientists who focus their attention on governments, political parties, interest groups, and the activities of people within them. Fourth, one can use, enjoy, and appreciate cultural objects; people live in houses. While sociologists have studied all of the social processes, they have concentrated their attention on the processes of appreciating cultural objects. Thus, sociologists focus their attention on the family, religious organizations, the community, medical organizations, and recreation. The general characteristics of all social processes form the study of social organization, while the various relations among cultural objects and social processes form the study of civilization, or the human condition.

Social processes are structured by roles. Whether he is an economist, a student of education, a political scientist, a sociologist, or a student of organization, the student of social process investigates the ways in which human beings accomplish tasks or perform actions. Because the student of social process investigates culture in action, he cannot view role, like the anthropologist, as a known set of rights and duties that the individual can accept or reject in a particular situation. The anthropologist sees role as a recipe for action. Thus, a person in school can know the role of student without performing it. For the student of social process, role is a set of actually expected behaviors relating to the performance of a function in accomplishing a task. The individual in a situation performs several operations with respect to his own actions. He adjusts his actions to what he expects others to do, to what he believes others expect him to do, and to the attainment of goals. For example, a student adjusts his actions to a teacher's grading policy, what he believes the teacher requires of him, and his goal of receiving an acceptable grade.

The differences between the concept of role in anthropology and the concept of role in the study of social processes can be illustrated by continuing the example of the teacher and student relation. For the anthropologist

THE HOUSE THAT JACK * BUILT (IN SUBURBIA)

1. THE HOUSE IS A CULTURAL OBJECT WITH A CERTAIN DESIGN AND LOCATION [RANCH HOUSE IN TICKY-TACKY TOWN]: <u>ANTHROPOLOGISTS</u> STUDY CULTURAL OBJECTS.

2. THE HOUSE WAS BUILT AND PAID FOR: <u>ECONOMISTS</u> STUDY THE PRODUCTION AND DISTRIBUTION OF CULTURAL OBJECTS.

3. JACK LEARNED HOW TO BUILD THE HOUSE: STUDENTS OF <u>EDUCATION</u> STUDY HOW PEOPLE LEARN ABOUT CULTURAL OBJECTS.

4. THE LAW SAID THAT JACK COULD NOT HAVE AN OUT-HOUSE IN HIS BACK YARD: <u>POLITICAL SCIENTISTS</u> STUDY HOW RULES ARE MADE AND ENFORCED IN COMMUNITIES.

5. JACK WATCHES FOOTBALL ON T.V. AND DRINKS BEER HAPPILY EVER AFTER (WITH HIS WIFE AND KIDS) IN THE HOUSE: <u>SOCIOLOGISTS</u> STUDY THE USES OF CULTURAL OBJECTS IN FAMILIES AND COMMUNITIES.

* AND SEVERAL MILLION OTHERS INCLUDING SALESMEN, FACTORY WORKERS, MINERS, TRUCK DRIVERS, EXECUTIVES, FRIENDS, AND...

there are one or more available role definitions present in the culture. The individual in a situation chooses to accept a given definition, to reject it, or to redefine it. Thus, a professor may accept the rule of grading on the basis of examination performance, reject it and base his grades on preference for personalities, or make a new rule that students grade themselves. In the actual process of education, however, some role definitions will be used by the participants as bases for guiding their behaviors. These definitions are not necessarily the same for all participants. One's belief about the expectations of others may be false, as may his expectations about what others will do. A student may expect his professor to center the course around examinations, while the professor may actually be concerned with deemphasizing testing and grading. The professor may expect students to compete vigorously for high grades, while the students may cooperate and pool their resources. Often when such differences between expectations are recognized, one actor adjusts his expectations to the other's role definition or the several actors bargain for a compromise. Thus, a student may change his expectations about the importance of examinations when he notices that the professor does not care much about them, or the professor may give more importance to examinations when he finds that students expect them to be significant. These adjustments do not always take place. Different actors may stick to conflicting role definitions as a matter of principle. One means of inducing social change is to act out a preferred role definition in spite of the expectations of others.

The anthropological view of role cannot fully account for the events that occur in social processes. Anthropologists describe known definitions of rights and duties. Students of social processes describe the fates of these definitions when they become premises of action in human relations. Sociologists, economists, political scientists, and students of education describe culture in action. They describe the expectations actually held by various participants in social processes and analyze what happens in the resulting interaction. From the anthropological view of role it is not possible to discover whether one definition of role will be accepted by all participants, whether there will be a compromise among different definitions, whether there will be continuing conflict, or whether entirely new definitions of role will be devised. The view of role as expected behavior, held by students of social processes, enables one to investigate the fates of role definitions when they are enacted in various situations.

The definition of social process implies that there are four main kinds of roles. Economic roles define expectations concerning the creation, preservation, destruction, and distribution of cultural objects. Houses are built by construction workers, financed by bankers, and paid for by consumers. Political roles define expectations about the ways in which decisions will be made to allocate time, space, and resources to using different cultural objects. Zoning laws are passed by local officials and enforced by housing inspectors or police. Educational roles define expectations concerning the communication of information about how to use cultural objects. People learn how to read blueprints, contracts, and instruction booklets from teachers. Appreciative roles define expectations about how cultural objects will be utilized or consumed. Husbands are often expected to take care of the family car and wives to cook the meals, although this may be changing. One should not think that these expectations are always well defined or that one consistent network of expectations characterizes each phase of a social process. In specialized and complex cultures, social processes are continuously changing. For example, the women's liberation movement has challenged the traditional role of wife by demanding equal employment opportunities and day-care centers for children.

ROLES AND HUMAN RELATIONS

The idea of role implies that more than one role exists. This statement can be explained by recalling how people are socialized, how they learn roles. First, the child finds the role an external constraint on his pursuit of satisfaction. Second, the child learns to judge his own actions by imagining how another particular person would judge them. The child can ask, "What would my mother think of this?" At this point the child receives his first intimation of his role as a child. However, he comes to understand that role only because there is a role of mother containing behaviors expected from the child and behaviors owed to the child. Thus, there would be no role of child without a role of adult. The child does not know his role except as reflected in the expectations of his mother or of other adults to whom he relates. Sociologist C. H. Cooley applied the term *looking-glass self* to the process of learning one's role as a reflection in the expectations of another role player.

Cooley believed that roles were generally mutually reacting or reciprocal systems. Following the example of the teacher and student relation, the teacher is expected to pass on knowledge about a subject and the student is expected to learn the material and to avoid interfering with the educational process. They are in a *cooperative* relation because they work together to fulfill the goals of the educational process. However, not all the relations defined by systems of roles are cooperative. In the educational process the relation between student and student is frequently defined as *competitive*. The student is expected to strive to gain higher grades and more honors than his fellows. Rules stating expected human relations are built into roles. With respect to the professor, it is expected that the student cooperate in his education. With respect to fellow students, it is expected that the student compete for grades and honors. Cooperation and competition are ways of achieving goals in social processes. People cooperate or compete with one another to reach goals such as knowledge or high grades.

Cooperation and competition are not the only major human relations. People also engage in conflict and love one another. In *conflict* one acts to prohibit another person from realizing a goal, while in *love* one acts to aid another person in achieving a goal. Conflict and love also occur in the educational process. In certain schools, particularly in ghetto and slum areas, the role expectations in the student-teacher relation contain conflict. The teacher expects the students to cause disorder and the students expect the teacher to despise them and to punish them. They fulfill one another's expectations and conflict occurs. Love can also arise in the educational process, as when teachers take extra time to help their students and when students do unsought favors for the teacher. Love does not ordinarily occur in the role expectations in the educational process, but in some places a tradition of cooperation can grow into expectations of love. In this context love should not be confused with raw emotion. To love, one must first take the role of the other and then enhance it. In conflict one attempts to destroy the role of the other. Competition and cooperation also involve taking the role of the other. In competition one attempts to perform a role better than the other performs the same role. In cooperation one attempts to contribute a necessary performance to the completion of a joint task. He must take the role of the other to learn how best to make his contribution. These examples show why students of human relations are called social psychologists. They investigate relations among human beings, which are social occurrences. They also study the motivations of human beings, which are psychological events.

ROLES AND PERSONALITY

Roles not only start relations among human beings, they also cause relations within the human personality. Since the human being is a possible creator of new rules, he is far from existing as a bundle of roles. However, since he performs many roles each day, his self-evaluation and plans for the future will be influenced by his role performances. At the center of the human world is the "I," judging the social actions of the "me" and drafting new plans for future actions. The "I" does not strive to satisfy all organic impulses, nor does it attempt to see that all relevant social roles are done efficiently. The "I" is an activity, integrating as far as possible the various parts of the "me" into a distinctive way of life. The "I" also plans for a future that may contain new ways of living not yet known to other people.

Often the integration of social roles into a distinctive way of life is difficult, if not impossible. This is the case because roles frequently contain vital contradictions. A man's personality may be split among his various roles. At work he may be expected to behave as a submissive employee, while at home he may be expected to take charge of a family. What kind of person is he if he is submissive for eight hours a day and authoritative for another eight hours? Can he unite these roles in a distinctive way of life? Further, even a single role can contain vital contradictions. The teacher is expected to win the confidence of his students so that they will be open to learning, but he is also expected to judge them through grading. Is the teacher a companion in learning or a judge? It is difficult to bring together these two expectations.

Psychologists study the ways in which human beings organize their various roles into ways of life, or personalities. They view human existence mainly from the perspective of the "I" rather than the perspective of the "me," which is the vantage point of anthropologists, sociologists, political scientists, economists, students of education, and social psychologists. Twentieth-century social thought has been a dialogue between students of the "I" and students of the "me," just as personal existence is a dialogue between man as role maker and man as role player (performing a role) and role taker (understanding another's role). As the discussion proceeds, it is important to remember the lesson from Mead that human beings actively create their culture only after they have learned about their possibilities in social relations. This principle will enable one to keep the whole in mind as he studies the parts.

SUMMARY

The social sciences study the dialogue, or conversation, between the creative "I" and the social "me." The social self ("me") can be understood as a bundle of roles which the person has gained through social learning. Each of the social sciences views role in a different way. In anthropology, roles are sets of rights and duties relating to the performance of a task. For any task there can be competing roles. For example, the role of teacher can be defined as resource person and counselor, or as judge. In the study of social processes, roles are sets of actual expectations relating to the performance of a task. Some of the rights and duties are put into action. In some schools teachers are expected to be judges and nothing else. Economists study the roles involved in producing and distributing cultural objects. Political scientists study the roles involved in making and enforcing rules regarding the use of cultural objects. Students of education discuss the roles involved in giving information about cultural objects. Sociologists study the roles involved in appreciating or using cultural objects in group situations. When roles are put into action, people form relations such as cooperation, competition, conflict, and love. Social psychologists study these relations. Roles are also made part of the self. The way they are fitted together into personalities is studied by psychologists. Psychologists also study how the "I" is expressed in action.

Central to the social sciences is the idea of culture, the material out of which the social self is composed. Anthropology, the study of culture, is the concern of the next chapter.

Notes

[1] Arthur F. Bentley, *The Process of Government* (Cambridge: Belknap Press of Harvard University Press, 1968), p. 4.

[2] David L. Miller, *Individualism* (Austin: University of Texas Press, 1967), pp. 42-43.

[3] *Ibid.*, p. 54.

[4] Arnold W. Green, *Sociology* (New York: McGraw-Hill Book Company, Inc., 1964), p. 134.

[5] A. L. Kroeber, *Anthropology: Culture Patterns and Processes* (New York: Harcourt Brace Jovanovich, Inc., 1963), p. 8.

[6] *Ibid.*, p. 10.

[7] Clifford Geertz, "The Impact of the Concept of Culture on the Concept of Man," in Yehudi A. Cohen (ed.), *Man in Adaptation: The Cultural Present* (Chicago: Aldine Publishing Co., 1968), p. 24.

Suggested Readings

Goffman, E. *The Presentation of Self in Everyday Life*, Garden City: Doubleday & Company, Inc., 1959 (paper).

Goodman, P. *Growing Up Absurd: Problems of Youth in the Organized Society*, New York: Random House, Inc., 1956 (paper).

Koestler, A. *The Ghost in the Machine*, New York: The Macmillan Company, 1967.

Wiener, N. *The Human Use of Human Beings: Cybernetics and Society*, New York: Avon Books, 1967 (paper).

CHAPTER TWO: THE ANTHROPOLOGIST'S PERSPECTIVE

Anthropologists are concerned with the study of culture. During the twentieth century the concept of culture has been central in discussions about the structure and forces of human existence. For this reason the word *culture* has been defined in many different ways by modern social scientists and philosophers. This book will use the definition of culture suggested by the anthropologist A. L. Kroeber: "Culture . . . is always first of all the *product* of men in groups: a set of ideas, attitudes, and habits—'rules' if one will—evolved by men to help them in their conduct of life."[1]

CONSEQUENCES OF CULTURE AS HUMAN PRODUCT

The anthropologist Albert Carl Cafagna has found several different uses of the term culture in the scholarly literature, each one of which is implied in Kroeber's definition of culture as a human product.

First, culture is defined as the social heritage of a group of human beings. In this sense, culture is a collection of ideas, rules, and material objects that have been created by human beings in the past and are now available for their use. Second, culture is defined as learned behavior. Unlike other animals, human beings cannot survive without learning ways of coping with such basic problems as acquiring food, clothing, and shelter. Culture seen as learned behavior involves the transmission of the social heritage.

Culture can be viewed as a system of ideas common to a group of human beings. This way of looking at culture highlights the fact that when people learn how to use their social heritage, they learn about the world and the ways of coping with the problems it presents. The knowledge that they acquire is in the form of ideas about what objects exist and how to act with reference to those objects. These ideas are recipes for action. For example, the idea that students are responsible for maintaining order in campus demonstrations is a recipe for action. Campus police may arrest those students who fail to maintain order.

Culture can also be viewed as shared behavior. This way of looking at culture is closely related to the view of culture as a system of ideas. The ideas that are contained in the social heritage and are transmitted to successive generations of human beings concern ways of acting with reference to objects. For example, students may translate the idea that they are responsible for maintaining order in demonstrations into concrete actions. They may select marshals to maintain crowd control and calm down those among them who get excited. In this example, the idea and the shared behavior fit together nicely. This is not always the case. Demonstrations have sometimes become riots, in which members of the crowd have forgotten the responsibility of maintaining order. Thought and action are not always in harmony. They are most likely to be in harmony when behavior or action is highly standardized.

Culture is a selection from all human behavior. Human activity appears limitless in its complexity, and the social scientist can only select parts of it for study. Selection occurs in everyday life as well as in social science. Students ordinarily define and evaluate their classroom experiences in terms of learning, but they may also make friends and enemies in classes, and some classes may change their goals in life. Thus, the definition and evaluation of classroom experiences in terms of learning is a selection from the total activity that occurs in classes. The ideas and standardized behaviors identified by anthropologists are selections from the total activity of the group. The core of culture is the role: a rule for using objects and for acting with reference to others. Ideas are the forms in which these rules are held by human beings and standardized behaviors are activities in agreement with rules. A standardized behavior is one that follows standards or rules. Since all human behavior does not follow rules, culture is a selection from behavior.

Culture is *superorganic*. It cannot be accounted for fully in terms of biological processes. The social heritage of a group must be separated from the biological heritage that characterizes a person as an organism. The idea that culture is superorganic is related to the debate about whether heredity or environment determines human behavior. Kroeber, who coined the term *superorganic*, was interested in making the study of culture separate from the study of biology, the organic. He argued that the organic processes of human beings placed limits on the range and character of their activities, while the social heritage determined activities within these limits. For example, human beings are organically incapable of flying without the aid of machines. The kinds of aircraft (superorganic) that they produce will determine how fast and far they fly.

In this text the simple division of human existence into organic and superorganic is not accepted. The human being is made up of four parts. The person is a biological organism; a participant in social relations; an organizer, creator, transmitter, and appreciator of culture; and a maker of the future. The strict division of human existence into organic and superorganic fails to recognize the major distinction between the social self ("me") and the creative self ("I"), as well as the division of the social self into elements of social process and culture. Calling everything human that is different from biological process the superorganic is an attempt to make the study of culture a complete social science. This would mean that sociology, economics, political science, education, social psychology, and psychology are only branches of anthropology. However, this is not accurate, because the concept of culture only refers to that part of the social self made up of well defined meanings and roles. The actual expectations of people in social relations often differ from the recipes, and human beings are capable of creating new recipes. Anthropology is important because it studies the contributions of the past to human existence in the present. However, the present and future are of equal importance to the past.

One of the most important parts of culture is the symbol.[2] Anthropologist Leslie A. White, who has emphasized the importance of symbols in human existence, defines a *symbol* as "a thing the value or meaning of which is bestowed upon it by those who use it."[3] Thus, a symbol is a physical thing with a meaning. The physical thing can be seen through the senses because it has color, sound, odor, taste, and texture. The meaning cannot be observed, but only can be understood by those who have learned it. An example of a symbol is the use of a red light to mean that one should stop his car at an intersection. The red light can be seen through the senses, but the meaning that one should stop his car must be learned. White points out that symbols are always somewhat arbitrary, selected without any particular reason. There is no reason red must be used to mean stop and green must be used to mean

A SYMBOL IS A PHYSICAL THING WITH A MEANING

go. Green could just as easily be used to mean stop, as could any other color. Nor must a color be used at all. Conceivably traffic could be controlled through sounds or smells; it is frequently controlled by the hand signals of policemen.

An important aspect of White's definition is that a symbol's meaning is given to it by those who use it. Dogs can be taught to respond consistently to words or physical motions. However, for the dog these words or motions are signs rather than symbols. White defines a *sign* as "a physical form whose function is to indicate some other thing—object, quality, or event."[4] A dog can be taught to fetch objects like slippers or a newspaper upon hearing a word. The word acts as a stimulus to the action of fetching. In a similar way, many human beings respond to the stimulus of a red light by stopping their cars without thinking of why they do it—the symbol of a red light has become a sign for them. However, there is an important difference between the dog and the human being. While both dog and man can respond to signals, the "man differs from the dog—and all the other creatures—in that *he can and does play an active role in determining what value the vocal stimulus is to have, and the dog cannot.*"[5] While the dog cannot decide which sound will stimulate him to fetch a newspaper, the human being can decide which color will mean stop. White observes that the creative faculty of "freely, actively, and arbitrarily bestowing value upon things, is one of the most commonplace as well as *the* most important characteristic of man."[6] He remarks that all culture depends upon the symbol. The use of the symbolic power brought culture into existence and the use of symbols makes it possible to transmit the social heritage.

The idea that culture is dependent upon symbols aids in understanding that culture is made up of rules evolved by men to help them in their conduct of life. Culture is a learned social tradition in the form of ideas and behaviors, growing from biological life and selected from the total mass of activity, which is dependent upon the human ability to create symbols. The important point is that ideas about the world and what actions to take in it are always expressed in symbols if they can be transmitted as part of culture. For example, traffic lights and road signs (symbols) are needed to inform drivers about hazards (ideas about the world) and laws (actions to take). It is through the use of symbols that human beings leave a legacy to future generations. The rights and duties defined in social roles are expressed in symbols. The social self ("me") is the center for organizing symbolic meanings and the creative self ("I") is the center for freely, actively, and arbitrarily bestowing value upon things. Cultural roles, or well defined sets of rights and duties relating to the performance of a task, can be learned because they are expressed in symbols, particularly the symbols of language. This is why the concept of symbol is so important in understanding the idea that culture is a set of rules evolved by men to help them in their conduct of life.

LANGUAGE

The most important symbols in human existence are those of language. Leslie White has dramatized the significance of language by showing the consequences of removing speech from culture. Speech is the kind of symbolizing that connects sounds with meanings. These meanings form a system, are common to a group of people, and allow these people to relate to the world, one another, and other cultural objects. The system of symbolic meanings common to a group of people is called a language. White remarks that several important consequences would follow from removing language from culture. First, there would be no human social organization, because human social organization depends upon the development of "I" and "me" components of the self. The "me" develops through the person taking the role of the other person in a social relation. The only way in which one can know the expectations of the other in a situation is symbolically, because expectations refer to events that are not being enacted in the present. A wife can expect that her husband will be happy to see her after a day's separation. Through language the person is able to symbolize the role of the other and to act with reference to his idea. The child is able to ask, "What will my mother think?" only by using language. Such roles as the generalized other, or the role of human being, are even more clearly dependent upon language. One never sees a human being act outside of particular circumstances. The generalized other is a selection from a number of situations, and it is only possible to understand it through language.

Apart from the dependence of social organization on symbols, tool-making and tool-using are also related to the human ability to create symbols. While Wolfgang Kohler succeeded in getting his chimpanzee Sultan to fit two sticks together and knock down a banana that he could not reach otherwise, there are problems of interpretation in this experiment.[7] Anthropologist Joseph H. Greenberg has criticized the claim that Kohler's experiment proves that non-human organisms are toolmakers: "While Sultan did produce an object that he did not find in his environment, the sticks had previously been fashioned by human carpenters to fit together. Without the prodding of the human experimenter, even Sultan would not have selected two sticks of his own accord and then put them together to form the tool he needed. At least, no nonhuman species has ever been observed to behave in this or in any comparable fashion on its own."[8] White remarks that "without articulate speech we would be all but toolless; we would have only the occasional and insignificant use of the tool such as we find today among the higher apes, for it was articulate speech that transformed the nonprogressive tool-using of the ape into the progressive, cumulative tool-using of man, the human being,"[9] Greenberg agrees with this judgment. He finds toolmaking and speech related in two basic ways. First, both processes have in common indirectness of action on the environment. Through tools, "man extends the sphere of his action through manipulation of some physical object that is not part of his own body," while through speech, "man can bring a fellow human being to do something for him."[10] For example, with a gun a man may get a person to hand over his money. The man may also get the money by using words to persuade the person to contribute to a "good cause." Second, beyond the simplest stages, toolmaking requires imaginative constructions of the characteristics and uses of the tool, or planning. A blueprint is drawn before a house is built. There can be no such planning in the absence of symbols. Thus, neither human social organization nor technology would be possible without the human ability to create and respond to symbols. Therefore, the process of symbolizing is basic to the development of the human self and central to the study of culture.

The symbols of speech are combined into a system called a language. Thus, each everyday language provides a distinctive way of interpreting human experience because no two languages symbolize exactly the same objects, or relate these objects together in the very same ways. The anthropologist Benjamin Lee Whorf was most responsible for pointing out the significant role of language in building human experience. Whorf argued that without language the human being sees the world as a kaleidoscopic flow of impressions, or a meaningless stream of colors, sounds, odors, tastes, and feelings. These sense qualities are organized into meaningful patterns only through language. Whorf held that we "cut nature up, organize it into concepts, ascribe significances as we do, largely because we are parties to an agreement to organize it in this way—an agreement (implicit and unstated) that holds throughout our speech community and is codified in the patterns of our language."[11] Since languages select only some experiences out of the continuous flow of impressions, each language gives its speakers a different overall view of the world. Gerald D. Berreman has supported Whorf's views: "Thus we know that people of different cultures categorize colors in different ways despite the fact that the visual stimuli they categorize are in all cases the same. Some name more colors than we do, some less. Other cultures do not place the boundaries between named colors exactly where we do."[12] What applies to colors also applies to other sense qualities, objects in the environment, supernatural beings, and human relations. However, this does not mean that because languages form experience a person cannot have experiences beyond those included in his language. Human beings are always having experiences that are not caught in the net of their language. Mainly, these experiences go unrecognized because there is no symbol by which they can be identified. If the human being were only composed of an organic and a social self ("me"), all experiences not covered by symbols would occur without recognition. However, the human being is also an "I," capable of naming new experiences. The center of the creative process in human beings is providing names for new experiences.

PATTERNS OF CULTURE

Although it is very important, language is only one part of culture defined as the rules evolved by men to help them in their management of life. Some anthropologists hold that languages express and shape distinctive views of man and his world. Similarly, many anthropologists claim that entire cultures form patterns that express distinctive ways of life or designs for living.

In Chapter I it was stated that the anthropologist sees roles as sets of rights and duties relating to the carrying out of a function in accomplishing a task. Rights are claims on other role performers for resources and actions necessary for accomplishing a task, and duties are obligations to provide other role performers with resources and actions so that they can perform their functions effectively. Anthropologists who claim that cultures form designs for living hold that the various role definitions in a culture are combined by underlying and fundamental principles. These principles express patterns of culture.

The anthropologist E. A. Hoebel has emphasized the idea that cultures express designs for living. He observes that just as languages select only certain experiences for naming out of the total continuous flow of impressions, so do entire cultures represent selections of only a few behavior patterns out of all possible human activities. Hoebel argues that the choice of behavior patterns, or roles, within a culture is not haphazard. It proceeds according to what he calls "fundamental cultural postulates."[13] Every culture is described by both existential and normative postulates.

Existential postulates are general statements about the nature of the external world and the nature of man. They are called *existential* because they are statements about what is, or what exists. For example, a culture could be united by the existential postulates that the universe is made up only of matter and that human beings are animals capable of using tools to further their survival as individuals and in groups. Postulates or statements such as these help integrate, or unite, the cultures of Soviet Russia and the nations of Eastern Europe.

Normative postulates are statements about what things and acts are good and to be sought after, or bad and to be rejected. For example, in Soviet

Russia and the nations of Eastern Europe investment in tools is judged good and changing fashions frequently is judged bad. Hoebel states that "existential and normative postulates are the reference points that color a people's view of things, giving them their orientation toward the world around them and toward one another."[14]

Hoebel remarks that the basic postulates of a culture are the same among themselves and that the people to whom they apply may or may not consciously believe them. This observation may be true for the small groups of preliterate people, or people who haven't yet learned to read or write, traditionally studied by anthropologists, but it is dangerous to extend it to large groups with complex cultures like the American people. In modern social existence different sets of basic postulates may clash with one another. Just as culture is an arena for debate among people offering different definitions of role, it is also an arena for debate among people holding different sets of fundamental, or basic, postulates. The two debates meet in disagreements about the definition of the role of generalized other, or the role of human being. The role of human being contains the fundamental normative and existential postulates.

There are dangers in taking too strict an interpretation of fundamental postulates in discussing a complex culture. These dangers are illustrated by Hoebel's attempt to spell out the world view for the people of the United States. He states that there are four fundamental parts of the American world view: rationalism and mechanism, pragmatic empiricism, individual-centeredness, and status and social mobility. *Rationalism-mechanism* is the doctrine that the universe is a physical system that operates according to laws discoverable by science. Human beings who understand these laws can partially control their environment by designing machines to solve their problems. Faith in the lawful universe and machine technology goes along with an attitude that things will work out for the best if one applies enough effort. *Pragmatic empiricism* is the doctrine that knowledge of how to accomplish activities is more important than traditional wisdom, general principles, or scientific descriptions of the relations among events. This view is consistent with the faith in machines but seems to clash with the belief in the universe as operating by scientific laws. *Individual-centeredness* is the doctrine that the individual human being is given primary responsibility for his development and is the proper reason for social activity. This means that Americans supposedly do not approve of the state taking care of human beings by giving them welfare payments, agricultural price supports, government contracts, or social security checks. *Status and social mobility* refer to the goals of moving up the social ladder by gaining the respect of fellow human beings. According to Hoebel, actual achievement rather than one's family background is the basis for respect in the United States. Achievement is measured by the amount of money one makes, because money is the means of obtaining consumer goods which allow one to demonstrate his status to others. For Hoebel, the fundamental existential postulates of American culture are rationalism-mechanism and pragmatic empiricism, while the fundamental normative postulates are individual-centeredness and status-social mobility. In Hoebel's view, the American believes that he can control his environment through the use of machinery and that he should use this control to further individual development, defined as obtaining higher status. The role of the human being in America is to rise in the social ladder through taking part in the technological society.

Hoebel's definition of the fundamental postulates of American culture is subject to important criticism. Ever since World War II there has been a growing challenge to the postulates identified by Hoebel. This challenge has come from spokesmen for minority groups such as blacks, Spanish-Americans, and American Indians; from youth movements such as beatniks and hippies; and from radical political movements of the left and right. Each of these groups challenges the fundamental postulates from different points of view. But overall their criticisms seem to replace machine technology with a concern for nature, practical knowledge with significance of emotional experience, individual development with a quest for deeper human relations, and competitive achievement of status with solidarity of the group. Whether or not this challenge will be successful cannot be predicted. It is important to mention it here because it causes doubt about the statement that American culture is characterized by a single set of fundamental existential and normative postulates.

The idea of cultural pattern was first applied to small groups of preliterate people. In such groups there is a much greater chance that a single set of fundamental postulates will apply than in a present-day complex culture. A good example of a world view that differs from views dominant in most of the United States is that of the Hopi Indians of the Southwestern United States. The Hopis are agricultural people who believe that the universe is a living whole, each part of which is complexly balanced with the others. The whole develops according to a single law and works for the good of the community. The role of the human being is to cooperate with his fellows in maintaining the balance of the whole through performing his appointed work

CULTURAL POSTULATES DETERMINE THE FORM OF LIFE

AMERICANS

HOPI

AMERICANS	HOPI
FAITH IN MACHINES	FAITH IN NATURE
+	+
FAITH IN SCIENCE	FAITH IN ANCIENT WISDOM
+	+
INDIVIDUAL RESPONSIBILITY	GROUP RESPONSIBILITY
+	+
CLIMBING THE SOCIAL LADDER	CONTENTMENT WITH ONE'S LOT
= THE RAT RACE IN THE BIG CITY	= THE GOOD LIFE DOWN ON THE FARM

BUT YOU CAN'T KEEP 'EM DOWN ON THE FARM

WHY NOT?

WHY AREN'T YOU DOWN ON THE FARM?

and fulfilling ritual duties. Since the Hopis believe that individuals can upset the balance of nature and thereby cause evil rather than good, their world view is very different from that designated to Americans by Hoebel. Americans believe that human beings should interfere in nature with machine technologies. The Hopis would be quite suspicious of such interference. Americans believe that competitive achievement should be the goal of human action. Hopis believe that the goal should be cooperation. It is possible that the growing concern in the United States with ecology and environmental pollution will bring the fundamental postulates of Americans closer to those of the Hopis.

HISTORY, DATA, AND METHOD

Anthropologists come to their view of interpreting role systems as inter-related wholes from a long history of studying preliterate peoples around the world. The beginnings of anthropology in modern times came during the Age of Exploration in the fifteenth century and thereafter, when European adventurers embarked on voyages in search of trade routes and precious metals. As they ventured far from Europe, the explorers met people sharing cultures quite different from the cultures of Europe. Most often, the Europeans used their superior military technology to make these people work for them and to convert them to Christianity. However, some Europeans became fascinated by the differences among role systems and wrote down their observations of the practices in various groups. This was the beginning of cultural anthropology.

In the nineteenth century many scholars in Europe and the United States attempted to bring some order into the many observations of preliterate peoples collected by travelers over the preceding several centuries. Using the role definitions of Europe as a standard of excellence and progress, they tried to show the stages through which simple cultures evolved into more complex systems of roles. These "armchair anthropologists" concentrated on library research and held the simplistic belief that European culture was the advanced model toward which all other cultures developed. This belief went along with the idea that in their economic penetration of the rest of the world, Europeans had shouldered a white man's burden to bring progress to peoples lacking complex machines, economic competition, and Christianity.

In the twentieth century cultural anthropology has undergone a profound change. Before the nineteenth century, travelers gathered personal impressions haphazardly through direct observation. During the nineteenth century, armchair anthropologists compared the reports of travelers and classified them according to systems of development from underdeveloped to progressive. In the twentieth century, anthropologists have systematically gathered information on different role systems through observations they made while taking part in cultures. The new approach involved two drastic changes from the armchair method. First, anthropologists abandoned the assumption that the industrial West provided a standard of excellence against which all other cultures could be measured. In place of this assumption they acted on the assumption that every system of roles expressed a distinctive design for living and made sense to the people who followed it. They held that the primary purpose of the anthropologist was to understand the role definitions in different cultures and to describe how these definitions fit together into a pattern. Second, to accomplish this purpose anthropologists devised a new method called *participant observation*. Participant observation is similar to the traveler's method of direct observation, because the anthropologist leaves the library to meet directly people of other cultures. However, the traveler, using direct observation, judged what he saw and heard in terms of the categories and roles of Western European culture. The anthropologist, using participant observation, attempts to understand the role definitions of the people he studies as interrelated and meaningful wholes. Thus, the participant observer, through learning the language of a preliterate people, observing their activities, and even performing some of these activities, can grasp fundamental postulates such as the Hopi world view.

The anthropologist, using the method of participant observation, has followed the idea of taking the role of the other farther than anyone else in history. He has often attempted even to play the role of the other. Normally the process of human development proceeds through the stages of experiencing roles as external impositions, taking the role of a particular other, taking the role of someone standing in a general relation, taking the role of human being defined in a particular culture and creating new role definitions. The anthropologist adds another stage between the steps of taking the role of human being defined in one's particular culture and creating new role definitions. He adds the stage of taking roles outside of one's own culture. From the anthropologist one learns that the role of human being is not the same in every culture. Alan Dundes writes that without the anthropologist's contribution of taking roles in other cultures, the person may be "unable to see that his way of doing things is not necessarily *the* way of doing things, but rather only one of the several alternatives devised by man."[15] The understanding gained through anthropology frees the human being from *ethnocentrism*, the attitude that one's own culture is the best one in all areas and that other cultures are merely poor attempts to equal it. The importance of freeing oneself from the role definitions of a single culture is illustrated in the comparison of the American and Hopi world views. The Hopi world view, with its insistence on the importance of preserving the balance of nature, may be more useful than machine-oriented thinking in coping with the present world environmental crisis. Through taking the roles in other cultures, one learns both about those cultures and about how to free oneself from unresisting acceptance of role definitions.

CULTURAL RELATIVISM AND RELATIVITY

Anthropologists understand that if one wants to comprehend the role defini-tions in other cultures, he must accept them without prejudice. He cannot allow judging them in terms of his own role definitions to interfere with understanding them as part of a distinctive pattern of culture. For example, among the Eskimo, when an old person could no longer perform functions necessary to the group's survival, he was abandoned by the group or he left it voluntarily. Or, in some parts of India, when her husband died a woman would be burned on his funeral pyre. Both of these practices are condemned by most people in industrialized societies. However, the anthropologist attempts to understand them as parts of a wider pattern of culture. The Eskimo, who lived by hunting and were on the move frequently, could not survive if delayed by old people unable to make a contribution. The case of the Indian wife is more complex. She was killed so that she could accompany her husband and continue to serve him. Anthropologists point out that this might not be a sufficient explanation of the practice. In the parts of India where the practice applied there were no rules covering the remarriage of women. Therefore, a widow would not make a full contribution to the main-tenance and betterment of group life. Thus, indirectly and unknown to the Indians themselves, this practice served the same purpose as abandonment of unproductive old people among the Eskimo. Both practices eliminated people who could not contribute fully to group life. The meanings of parts of culture for the whole need not always be understood by the people who actually play roles.

Along with the growth of investigation in anthropology has gone an in-creasing challenge to the traditional moralities of Western Europe and the United States. When people learn that their way of doing things is not neces-sarily *the* way of doing things, but rather only one of the several alternatives devised by man, they begin to wonder whether it is possible at all to judge some role definitions better than others. There are several responses to the confusion caused by knowledge of the different role definitions around the world. First, one can say that despite all of the differences among role defini-tions, the definitions within his own culture are the best ones in all circum-stances. This response is a refusal to accept the contribution that anthropolo-gists make to freeing people from passive, or unresisting, acceptance of role definitions. Second, one can say that each culture is a distinctive design for living, suitable for the people who follow it. Since each part of the culture is closely interconnected with the rest, it is not possible to judge any part as bad. This response, called *moral relativism*, is just as misleading as the ethnocentric response. First, cultures are not fully integrated wholes, in which each part performs a necessary function in maintaining the entire system. Second, this view states that human existence is used up by the social self ("me") and that there is no creative self ("I") responsible for making new roles. Third, this view implies that a person can learn nothing important from other cultures to improve his conduct of life. Fourth, and most important, moral relativism confuses the acts of understanding and moral judgment. This last point deserves further discussion.

Moral relativists believe that because a person can understand the part that a role definition plays in maintaining a distinctive way of life, he must judge that role definition good or fitting for the people who perform it. This confuses taking the role of the other with judging the role of the other as good. Even though one understands the conscious and hidden purposes of killing a wife when her husband dies, he need not declare that this practice is desirable, even for the people using it. He need not say that the fundamental normative postulates of all cultures are equally good. He can point out that there are ways in which widows might improve group life. He might even say that attempts should be made to get the people to abandon their belief that a woman should be killed so that she can continue to serve her departed husband. To understand is not always to approve. One can understand why some people became Nazis without approving of their brutalities. *Moral relativity* is the position that while there are reasons for people playing widely different roles in different cultures, not all reasons are equally good from a moral point of view. As a scientist, the anthropologist is concerned primarily with discovering why people in different cultures play different roles. In this phase of his work, he does not judge role definitions as ethically good or bad. However, the anthropologist, with his wide knowledge of normative postulates, can attempt to identify general principles of moral judgment in another phase of his work. However, it is important that he keep the two phases of his work separate from one another, or he is apt to fall into the incorrectness of ethnocentrism or moral relativism. If he becomes a moral philosopher, the anthropologist must develop a standard for judging roles as good and bad. This standard, which might represent a combination of normative postulates from the cultures of the world, is as yet only a dim hope of some social scientists.

SUMMARY

The anthropologist studies culture, or a set of rules developed by men to help them in their conduct of life. These rules are organized into roles, or sets of rights and duties relating to the performance of a task. For the anthropologist, roles are recipes suggesting courses of action under various circumstances. They are not always followed in action, because human beings can reject traditional recipes and devise new ones. Especially in small preliterate societies, roles are organized into patterns of culture, or distinctive designs for living, which are unified by fundamental existential and normative postulates. As cultures become more complex, there is less unification by a single set of fundamental postulates. Frequently, several different sets of postulates compete for belonging in the cultural arena. Fundamental postulates are closely related to roles, because they are central in defining the role of human being in a group.

Anthropologists learn about patterns of culture by taking the role of the other in cultures different from their own. By showing people how to go beyond the judgments of their own cultures, anthropologists make an important contribution to human freedom and civilization. However, their work should not be misunderstood to mean that all roles are equally good. Moral judgment is not the same as cultural understanding, and a person cannot escape his responsibility to judge by saying that just because people play a role it is a good role. The creative self ("I") has the capacity to judge among the roles of the social self ("me"). When anthropology is understood properly it is an aid to the creative self rather than a rejection of it. It frees the self from the bondage of ethnocentrism and enables it to become a more conscious creator of role definitions.

Notes

[1] A. L. Kroeber, *Anthropology: Culture Patterns and Processes* (New York: Harcourt Brace Jovanovich, Inc., 1963), p. 10.

[2] Albert Carl Cafagna, "A Formal Analysis of Definitions of Culture," in Gertrude E. Dole and Robert L. Caneiro, (eds.), *Essays in the Science of Culture in Honor of Leslie White* (New York: Thomas Y. Crowell Company, 1960), pp. 111-132.

[3] Leslie A. White, "The Symbol: The Origin and Basis of Human Behavior," in Jesse D. Jennings and E. Adamson Hoebel, (eds.), *Readings in Anthropology* (New York: McGraw-Hill Book Company, Inc., 1966), p. 288.

[4] *Ibid.*

[5] *Ibid.*, p. 289

[6] *Ibid.*, p. 290

[7] Wolfgang Kohler, *The Mentality of Apes* (New York: Random House, Inc., 1956).

[8] Joseph H. Greenberg, *Anthropological Linguistics* (New York: Random House, Inc., 1968), p. 4.

[9] Jennings and Hoebel, *Readings*, p. 292.

[10] Greenberg, *Anthropological Linguistics*, pp. 4-5.

[11] Ralph L. Beals and Harry Hoijer, *An Introduction to Anthropology* (New York: The Macmillan Company, 1965), p. 634.

[12] Gerald D. Berreman, "Ethnography: Method and Product," in James A. Clifton, (ed.), *Introduction to Cultural Anthropology* (New York: Houghton Mifflin Company, 1968), pp. 366-367.

[13] E. Adamson Hoebel, *Anthropology: The Study of Man* (New York: McGraw-Hill Book Company, Inc., 1966), p. 23.

[14] *Ibid.*

[15] Alan Dundes, (ed.), *Every Man His Way* (Englewood Cliffs: Prentice-Hall, Inc., 1968), p. vii.

Suggested Readings

Childe, V. G. *Man Makes Himself*, New York: New American Library of World Literature, Inc., 1952 (paper).

Firth, R. *Human Types*, New York: New American Library of World Literature, Inc., 1958 (paper).

Hall, E. T. *The Silent Language*, New York: Fawcett World Library, 1969 (paper).

Hays, H. R. *From Ape to Angel: An Informal History of Social Anthropology*, New York: G. P. Putnam's Sons, 1964 (paper).

Henry, J. *Culture Against Man*, New York: Random House, Inc., 1963 (paper).

Kroeber, A. L. and Kluckhohn, C. *Culture: A Critical Review of Concepts and Definitions*, New York: Random House, Inc., 1952 (paper).

Mead, M. *Sex and Temperament*, New York: Dell Publishing Co., Inc., 1967 (paper).

Tax, S. editor, *Horizons in Anthropology*, Chicago: Aldine Publishing Company, 1964 (paper).

Whatmough, J. *Language: A Modern Synthesis,* New York: New American Library of World Literature, Inc., 1956 (paper).

CHAPTER THREE: CULTURAL DIVERSITY AND CONFLICT

Anthropologists have been among the people most responsible for increasing human awareness of cultural differences. Organizing and clearing up the more haphazard observations of travelers and armchair scholars, they have shown that throughout the world definitions of roles vary widely. Before the interference of industrial technology, American law, Christianity, and mass produced consumer goods into Eskimo life, the role of the old person in Eskimo culture was different from the role of the old person in the culture of most Americans. Before Britain gained political and economic supremacy in India, the role of the Indian wife was different from the role of the English wife. The Eskimo subjected old people to exposure outside when they could no longer perform a useful function for the group, and in some sections of India wives followed their husbands to death by fire on the funeral pyre. When

Americans, Englishmen, and other Europeans came across these practices and others like them, there was an awareness of cultural differences. One of the most important events in recent history has been the growing recognition of differences within and between cultures. Responses to this recognition have frequently involved cultural conflicts. The significant cultural conflicts of the contemporary world involve struggles between religions (Catholics and Protestants in Northern Ireland), racial groups (blacks and whites in the United States), age groups (the generation gap and cultural "revolution" throughout the world), sex groups (the feminist movement), national groups (Arabs and Israelis), and many other rules and objects. Almost every conflict involves culture in the sense that it is about tools, symbols, rules and/or products. An examination of the major kinds of cultural diversity will lead to a better understanding of the structure of cultural conflict.

TYPES OF CULTURAL DIVERSITY

The Components of Culture

The major kinds of cultural objects, defined by their uses in human existence, are tools, symbols, products, and rules. The system of *tools* available to a group of human beings makes up the technology of that group. Technology is used to produce other objects of culture. Therefore, the *tool* is a cultural object used to produce another cultural object. An example of a tool is a pencil. It can be used to create symbols such as numbers and words, abstract or representational drawings, commands to other individuals and many other objects. Normally, one would not desire a pencil unless he planned to produce something with it.

The system of *symbols* available to a group of human beings makes up the communications system of that group. A communications system is used to transmit information about cultural objects and other things from one person to another. Therefore, the symbol is a cultural object used to refer to another cultural object or events in the physical and organic realms. An example of a symbol is the American flag. It is used to refer to the United States and all of the activities that go on within it. When an American flag appears on an airplane, people who understand the meaning of the symbol know that the plane belongs to the American government or an American corporation. A symbol is a thing whose value or meaning is given to it by those who use it.

The system of *products* available to a group of human beings comprises, or makes up, the goods and services of that group. Goods and services are used to produce experiences for human beings. Therefore, a *product* is an end result of other parts of culture. It combines the means for producing a desired experience or condition. Goods and services are sometimes called values because people desire them for the experiences brought by their use. An example of a good and service is medical care. Medical care is used to gain the experience and condition of good health. Similar to medical care in this respect is fine art, which is used to attain the experience of appreciating the beautiful.

THE HOUSE THAT JACK BUILT (REVISITED)

THERE ARE 4 COMPONENTS TO CULTURE

JACK USED A HAMMER (TOOL),

TO BUILD A DOG HOUSE (PRODUCT),

AFTER HE READ AN INSTRUCTION BOOK (SYMBOLS),

AND MADE SURE THE ZONING LAWS PERMITTED IT (RULES)

The system of *rules* available to a group of human beings makes up the organization or role system of that group. Roles are sets of rights and duties concerning access to cultural objects, uses of cultural objects, treatment of other human beings, and treatment of the physical and organic world. Therefore, the *rule* is a cultural object used to regulate the uses of other cultural objects. An example of a rule is the command, "Do not steal." It is used to guide human conduct with respect to the ownership of cultural objects and portions of the physical and organic realms. Taking the role of the other means understanding the rights and duties of the other with regard to the uses of nature and culture involved in accomplishing a certain task.

Depending upon its uses, the same object can be a tool, symbol, or product. For example, an automobile can be a tool for transporting people from place to place, a symbol of wealth or life style, or a way of gaining the experience of excitement. Distinctions among the major kinds of cultural objects are closely tied to the purposes served by these objects. However, each cultural object has a main use. A pencil is primarily a tool for producing symbols and art, even though it could be used as a symbol for a stationery store or as a good producing the experience of drawing. The American flag is primarily a symbol for a nation, even though it could be used as a tool in packing goods to prevent breakage or as clothing. A statue is primarily a good or product producing experience of the beautiful, even though it could be used as the symbol of a city or as a tool for breaking windows. A political constitution is primarily a system of rules, even though it could be used as a symbol for a nation.

Diversity and Cultural Components

Cultural systems vary according to each of the four major components. Technological components of different cultures vary according to how frequently machines are used in the production of goods, the type of energy used in production (manpower, beasts of burden, water, steam, fossil fuels, electricity, atomic power), and the type of goods produced (raw materials, manufactured products, synthetics). Followers of Karl Marx and many other Western thinkers believe that the technological component is the most important part of a cultural system. For them, the human being is primarily a toolmaker and tooluser. Thinkers who hold this central belief divide societies according to whether the primary economic activity is hunting and gathering, agriculture, manufacturing or, for some, processing information. Unless one holds the belief that the technological component is the most significant one, it is misleading to classify whole societies as merely agricultural or industrial, and as developed, developing, or underdeveloped. It is popular now to characterize the United States as a "technological society" in which the constant creation of new tools determines the quality of human existence. This overemphasis on tools obscures the fact that production issues in certain kinds of goods and services, is carried on in an organizational setting, and is coordinated through communication.

Communications systems of different cultures vary according to the degree to which symbolic systems are specialized, the experiences captured by symbols, and the sheer qualitative differences among symbols. Some cultures, like those of the contemporary West, have many and highly specialized symbolic systems. There are various mathematical systems used by scientists and engineers; liturgical languages like Hebrew, Latin, Greek and Slavonic, used by different religious groups; systems of slang used by age groups and ethnic groups; professional languages, such as those used by doctors, lawyers, and academicians; musical notation; Morse code; sign languages; simplified languages such as Pidgin English used for aiding economic exchange among different cultural groups; ideological languages used in movements for social change; ordinary language; and many other symbolic systems. Preliterate cultures are much less likely to have so much specialization in symbolic systems. The experiences captured in symbolic systems also vary among cultures. For example, the Eskimo have many words to characterize different kinds of snow, while English-speaking peoples must differentiate by adding adjectives to the word *snow*. The Eskimo is more likely to notice differences in snow than the American because his language gives him more available descriptive categories. Finally, languages differ in grammar and in the qualitative content of the symbols. Japanese has a different grammar from English, and it contains different symbols. Differences in the grammar and symbols of languages used in cultures with similar technological components shows that the technological component does not determine strictly every other cultural component.

Systems of goods and services in different cultures vary according to the variety of goods available, the part of goods concerned with food, clothing, and shelter, the part of goods devoted to private rather than group or community use, and the standardization of available goods. Contemporary Western cultures are characterized by a wide variety of available goods; many products not connected directly with providing food, clothing, and shelter; a high amount of goods devoted to private use; and highly standardized products. The opposite is true of preliterate cultures which are characterized by less variety in goods, less goods not directly connected with the satisfaction of physiological needs, less goods for private uses, and less standardization. It is by no means necessary that a culture with a technological component centered on electricity, machine production, and electronic data processing and communication must provide a wide variety of goods of which a high proportion are used privately and not connected directly with food, clothing, and shelter. The Soviet Union and Eastern European nations have provided a more restricted variety of goods for private uses than the nations of Western Europe or North America, although technological components are similar. Just as in the case of language, the kinds of products available in a culture are not uniquely determined by the technological component of that culture.

Systems of rules in different cultures vary according to the specialization of roles, the number of choices of role definitions for a certain task, and the way that people are judged fit or unfit to perform a role. In contemporary Western cultures roles are highly specialized, there are choices of definitions for many roles, and there are complex systems of judgment. In preliterate cultures, however, roles are relatively unspecialized, few roles have choices in definitions, and systems of judgment are simple. Of these standards for judgment the ways that people are judged fit or unfit to perform a role are particularly important. There are many possible measures for judgment, any or all of which may enter into an overall evaluation. For example, a person can be decided to be fit to play a role because he has performed certain tasks well. Thus, a person may be licensed as a doctor because he has passed an examination in medical skills and has reached a certain standard of achievement in medical school. Or, a person can be judged fit to play a role because he is a particular kind of person. Thus, a person may become a shaman, or medicine man, because his father was a medicine man. Many roles in contemporary Western cultures embody judgment in agreement with performance or achievement. However, it is a mistake to believe that achievement is the standard for all roles in any culture. In American society a husband and father is judged fit to perform his role if he provides a certain standard of living for his wife and children. The wife is judged fit to perform her role if she provides a certain standard of care for home, spouse, and children. However, the child is normally judged fit to perform his role simply by existing as the offspring of the parents. This is not the case in some sectors of American culture and in many other cultures where, after a certain age, the child is expected to make a direct contribution to the material well-being of the family. The tension between judgment according to performance and judgment according to a characteristic or quality of a person is highlighted by present cultural conflicts. For certain jobs in American society, a person is judged fit to perform a role according to achievement, as long as he is male, white, over twenty-one, and under sixty-five. This situation continues in spite of the passage of laws aimed at guaranteeing judgment according to achievement.

Like symbol systems and products, systems of rules or role-definitions are not uniquely determined by the technological component of a culture. While the technological components of Soviet and American cultures are similar, roles relating to the ownership and control of tools are quite different. In America, the role of stockholder is important in the organization of ownership, while it is of no relevance in the Soviet Union. Similarly, in the Soviet Union, the role of Communist Party member is significant in the control of production, while it is of no relevance in the United States. It is possible that systems of rules are important in determining the character of the technological component of a culture. At one time, economic competition, a matter of organization and not technology, may have encouraged the invention of machines. Today, budgeting funds for research and development may perform a similar role in encouraging innovation. Laws guaranteeing contract and granting patents were also important in technical innovation because they allowed people to profit from their inventions.

Diversity Within Cultures

Particularly in contemporary Western cultures, there are groups of people who use different tools, symbols, products, and rules from those widespread in the general culture. These groups form *subcultures* within the general culture.

Perhaps the most evident basis for differentiating subcultures in the contemporary West is occupation. Around the use of different tools, different styles of life grow up. Each occupation forms more or less of a community which is relatively closed and hostile to outsiders. Professional associations and unions appear to advance and protect the interests of occupational groups. Specialized languages are developed to name and organize experiences connected with the job. The members of the occupational group may even develop a characteristic consumption, or use, pattern. For example, in the United States medical doctors are expected to have a middle-class life style, are organized into several powerful professional associations, have a specialized language for diagnosis and treatment, and take more medicines than most Americans.

Use of specialized tools is not the only basis for the development of subcultures. People who speak a daily language different from the one most often spoken in the general culture, people who belong to a different religious faith from the majority, people who have different skin color from the majority, people of various age groups, people who consume different items, people of different sexes, and people who favor different definitions of role may form subcultures. It is frequently very difficult even to speak of a general culture in the contemporary Western world. As a whole, Western cultures may be held together by a widely accepted role of the human being.

However, even on the level of the role of human being, spokesmen for minority racial groups and militant youth groups have presented new definitions to compete with those most widely accepted. For example, some people in the black and youth movements favor replacing large organizations with local and community controlled units.

Subcultures can be more or less inclusive in their scope. Some occupational categories do not have very distinctive tools, are poorly organized, use the symbols of ordinary language, and are not associated with a characteristic consumption pattern. In such a case the occupational subculture is nearly nonexistent and has very little range beyond the job. Clerical and retail sales personnel have weak subcultures of this sort. Some occupational categories have distinctive tools, are well organized, have a characteristic consumption pattern, and follow a special code of rules. In such a case the occupational subculture is of great importance. Military officers in the West have traditionally had strong subcultures of this sort. They have paid allegiance to a code of honor and have been constrained by a special military law. They have not indulged in conspicuous consumption of luxuries, have specialized in the use of armaments, and have developed impressive means of action to protect their interests. It is important to distinguish among subcultures based on a specialized function and subcultures based on a general characteristic like an ordinary language or skin color. Subcultures based on a specialized function could not exist if other functions were not performed. Thus, there could be no military subculture if other groups did not provide food, clothing, and shelter. Subcultures based on a general characteristic could exist in the absence of other groups. Thus, all social tasks could be performed by the members of a single racial group. Cultural conflicts between specialized groups are not as severe and dangerous as those between general groups, because the different specialities need one another, while different language and racial groups could exist without one another, and may compete for the same goods. This is one reason why racial and linguistic minorities tend to become specialized in occupation, like American blacks who have concentrated in unskilled service work. The other and more important reason for occupational specialization is restriction of access to decent jobs by the dominant group.

Important cultural differences occur within cultures as well as between them. These differences comprise variations in tools, symbols, products, and rules. The wide diversity among cultures does not automatically lead to conflict, but some of the most serious contemporary conflicts are cultural. It is useful to inspect some of these conflicts with the four components of culture in mind.

CULTURAL CONFLICT

Conflict is a process of active disagreement among human beings or groups of people. Cultural conflicts occur when there is active disagreement over tools, symbols, products and/or rules. Actual conflicts vary according to the scope of culture involved and the means through which the disagreement is expressed. Accompanying cultural conflicts are opposing definitions of role, and such conflicts can be usefully understood by recalling the ways in which people learn roles.

People mature as they become able to take the role of the other with reference to their own action. The young child asks, "What would my mother think if I did this?" The older child asks, "What would an adult think if I did this?" The socialized person asks, "What would people think if I did this?" Thus, people become aware of their differences from others and, therefore, of their own personalities, by putting themselves in the place of others. One would not know himself as a particular human being unless he could compare himself to others. The same principle holds for groups of human beings. People would not realize that they were Americans unless they knew about the existence of other nations and could view America from the standpoint of another national group. One can have black skin without noticing it or making it special in any way. Before the European conquests black Africans were not aware of their skin color as something special. They doubtless thought of it in the same way that most people today think about the fact that they have five fingers. When everyone is black, no one takes black skin seriously, or even notices it. When white Europeans penetrated African cultures, skin color became socially and culturally significant. It became possible to distinguish among people on the basis of whether they were black or white, and to use that basis for assigning them to different social tasks. Thus, skin color became a basis for differentiating among roles. There were no natives, Africans, American Indians, Orientals, or aborigines before European and North American conquistadors devised these categories. There were people, existing in cultures, who were not aware that widely different life styles existed.

Contact among widely different cultural groups does not necessarily lead to the domination of one group by the other. However, when one group has more powerful tools, more differing products, more specialized symbol systems, and more efficient means of organization than the other, some kind of dominative relation is likely. Domination takes the form of taking natural resources and labor from the weaker group and assigning special roles to the weaker group. The process of domination displaces the tools, products, symbols, and rules of the weaker group in favor of the cultural objects of the stronger group. People in the weaker group are assigned roles seen as inferior by members of the stronger group. They may be employed as plantation workers, domestics, unskilled factory workers, porters, janitors, and other menial roles, as in the experience of black Americans. When there is cultural domination, the economic roles of the weaker group are integrated into the role system of the stronger group. This may even happen when the dominant group is a numerical minority. In South Africa a relatively small number of whites dominate a relatively large number of blacks.

RACISM

At the center of domination is a split in the definition of the role of human being. The stronger group makes two human roles, one for its own members and one for the members of the weaker group. The role of the human being defined for the stronger group likely includes judgments that people should be responsible actors and are capable of benefiting from maximum access to products, symbols and tools. The role of the human being defined for the weaker group probably includes judgments that the minority is hopelessly irresponsible and incapable of benefiting from access to high quality products, complex systems of symbols, and sophisticated tools. Thus, the dominant group devises two images of the human being. Sometimes the process goes as far as the declaration that the members of the weaker group are more like animals than people and are, therefore, not even entitled to be treated according to the same rules as those used for the stronger group. The two images of the human being provide the justification for rewarding members of one group and depriving members of the other group. Thus, members of the weaker group are not given jobs that involve the use of sophisticated tools because they are said to lack the responsibility and intelligence to use them well. Similarly, they are not given the means for getting high quality products because they are said to be unable to appreciate the finer things in life. They are given inferior education, or none at all, because they are said to be naturally stupid. They are given a special status under the law because they are said to be incapable of controlling themselves. All of these arguments have been used to justify discrimination against black Americans as well as many other minority groups. The splitting of the role of human being into two roles is a decisive aspect of contemporary cultural conflict.

Cultural domination may be based on any of a large number of factors. Sometimes race is the distinctive quality, but religious faith, linguistic group, nationality, or political persuasion have been the deciding factors at different places and times. At the present time, the same kind of inferior role assigned by some white Americans to blacks is assigned by North Irish Protestants to Catholics, by Nigerian Hausa tribesmen to Ibo tribesmen, by Vietnamese to Cambodians, by many English-speaking Canadians to French Canadians, and by some northern whites in the United States to southern whites. This leads to the question of whether or not the judgments contained in these roles have any basis in fact.

It is very difficult to prove whether or not the judgments contained in the role definition of members of the weaker group are true. Role definitions tend to be *self-fulfilling prophecies*, or statements that come true in part because they are believed. This is the case for two reasons. First, if the stronger group is convinced that members of the weaker group would not benefit from access to cultural objects, it will not provide them with the means to benefit from such objects. Many American blacks are not presently capable of correctly using sophisticated tools, fully enjoying philosophical novels, understanding integral calculus, or fathoming intricate legal procedures. This is not necessarily because they are stupid, but because they have not been given the educational opportunities of many whites. Grave doubts about inherent inferiority have resulted from studies begun during World War I which show that northern blacks in the United States gain higher scores on intelligence tests than southern whites.[1] Current debates over statistics that show blacks having slightly lower test scores than whites are of much less importance than commonly thought. Even if these test scores reflected differences in native ability, and it is by no means clear that they do, large numbers of blacks still score far higher than large numbers of whites. Thus, such statistics do not constitute any argument for treating members of different races in different ways, nor for according racial groups special images. If there are differences in native ability among racial groups, they are far less important than differences in cultural opportunity. The apparent differences among racial and other cultural groups are primarily the result of self-fulfilling prophecies. The member of the weaker group will never be able to prove himself unless he is given full opportunity. Race is a matter of cultural, not biological, definition.

AVERAGE INTELLIGENCE PROVES NOTHING ABOUT PARTICULAR PEOPLE

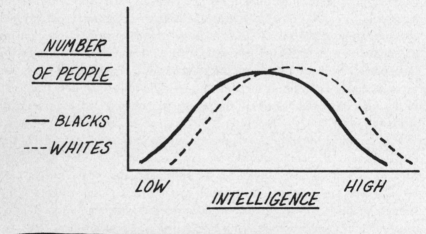

The self-fulfilling prophecy works in another even more subtle way. While the separate role of human being for members of the weaker group justifies discrimination by the stronger group, it also affects self-definitions in the weaker group. Some members of the weaker group begin to believe that they really are what the stronger group claims them to be. This reaction can be understood as a variant of taking the role of the other. In a situation of dominance, the actions of the stronger group are of vital importance to the fate of the weaker group. Through continued contact, members of the weaker group increasingly take the role of members of the stronger group and ask, "What would a member of the stronger group think if I did this?" Through this process of considering the judgments of the stronger group, members of the weaker group make the role definitions of the stronger group part of their social selves. The "me" becomes composed partly of the standards of the stronger group. The farther this process goes the more submissive do members of the weaker group become. At the extreme, members of the weaker group not only accept definitions of economic role enforced by the stronger group, but may also accept the special role of human being accorded to them. Thus, when the process is carried to its conclusion, members of the weaker group believe that they are irresponsible and incapable of using sophisticated tools, enjoying high quality products, understanding complex symbolic systems, and participating in political decisions. A large number of black Americans have historically accepted the role defined for them by whites. However, during the past half century, movements have arisen to shake this acceptance.

Sociologists Charles F. Marden and Gladys Meyer call the process in which members of the weaker group accept the role definitions of the stronger group "stabilized accommodation": "This mode of adaptation is one in which both superior and subordinate positions are taken for granted. Both dominant and minority members accept the same rationalizations for the existing pattern. Both may equally defend it."[2] If this is the case, how do conflicts of culture arise? The acceptance of domination by members of the weaker group may come into question in several ways. First, all members of the stronger group may not believe that the role of human being should be split into superior and inferior types. They may attempt to act on the principle that there is only one human role. When this is the case, the member of the weaker group has more than one way of taking the role of someone in the stronger group. While he may still accept splitting the role of human being, he also has the option of declaring that there is only one human role. If he rejects a special role, he is likely to come into conflict with members of the stronger group who intend to maintain a split role. He is also likely to get support from members of the stronger group who favor only one human role. Much of the conflict between black and white in the United States has followed this pattern. Many white Americans subscribe to the principle that all human beings are equal and, therefore, find it difficult to justify discrimination against blacks. Sociologist Gunnar Myrdal called this an "American dilemma."[3] The blacks are able to take advantage of white uncertainty to improve their positions. In this case cultural conflict is possible because of prior tensions in the culture of the stronger group.

Cultural conflict is possible, but much less likely, when the culture of the stronger group is unified in defining the role of human being as split. A second way in which cultural conflict occurs centers on tensions between the particular roles performed by members of the weaker group and the split role of human being. In performing tasks for the dominant group, members of the weaker group may be given responsibility and granted access to sophisticated tools, high quality products, complex symbolic systems, and even means of decision-making. The gap between the duties that they perform and the role of human being given to them may lead members of the weaker group to imagine themselves in the role of a member of the stronger group. This is not the same as taking the role of a member of the stronger group. In taking a role the person asks, "What would a member of the stronger group think if I did this?" He attempts to anticipate the judgment of the other and take the anticipation into account when he acts. When one imagines himself in the role of another, he acknowledges the possibility that he could play the imagined role. He asks, "What would life be like if I were a member of the stronger group?" Once he is capable of asking that question, the member of the weaker group need not accept the split role of human being. He can take the role of human being that the stronger group gives to its own members and ask, "What would a member of the stronger group think if I did this and I belonged to the stronger group?" Brewton Berry observes that at this stage genuine race relations appear because the member of the weaker group "feels that his inferior status in the new society is determined by his race and not by his culture which he shares with the dominant group."[4]

When the person is able to ask, "What would a member of the stronger group think if I did this and I belonged to the stronger group?," he no longer automatically accepts the split role of human being. He has several choices. He can accept the role of human being that the stronger group accords to its own members, and attempt to bring treatment into line with this role definition. This is the plan of integration and assimilation. It only succeeds if enough members of the stronger group are willing to let it succeed. The drive of the civil rights movement, the racial integration movement, and the movement for equal opportunity in the United States is an example of the strategy, or plan, of integration and assimilation. A second choice is to define a new role of human being for members of the weaker group based on role definitions present in the group historically. This is the strategy of separatism.

Many black Americans who want to revive and further create a black culture, and who find a quality of "soul" in blacks that is supposedly not present in whites, tend in the direction of separatism. At the present time in the United States, most blacks are neither fully integrationist nor fully separatist. They are integrationist in their demand for equal job opportunities, but separatist in their demand that black children learn particularly about black history.

Assimilation (absorption), separatism, or a balance between them are not the only possible strategies of cultural encounter. Members of the weaker group may accept the role of human being defined in a revolutionary doctrine and attempt to make it general in the culture. This appears to be the strategy of radical groups like the Black Panthers who favor creating a "new socialist man" after the society has been revolutionized. They claim that after the revolution both blacks and whites would share the same role of human being. Like the strategy of integration and assimilation, the revolutionary strategy involves the cooperation of members of the stronger group. Members of the weaker group may also reverse the split role of human being and declare that the stronger group is basically inferior to the weaker group. They may plan for the day when the weaker group will become dominant. This appears to be the strategy of the Black Muslims, many of whose members are convinced of black superiority.

Racism, assimilation, separatism, revolutionism, and reverse racism are all strategies that have been tried in the twentieth century. They have their counterparts in religious, linguistic, national, and regional struggles. None of them has been very successful in calming cultural conflicts. There is another strategy, transculturation, which has not yet been tried extensively. Transculturation involves creating a new role of human being out of the various definitions present in the several cultures in contact. Instead of debating whether blacks should accept white culture or whether they should pursue their separate development, white Americans might ask what phases of white and black culture should be combined in a new complete culture. The strategy of transculturation would involve a recognition by whites that there is much for them to learn from the cultures of minority groups, and a recognition by members of minority groups that they have something to contribute to a general culture. Certain youth groups in the United States have begun the process of transculturation by learning to appreciate the music of black Americans, the religious and philosophical system of the Orient, and even the drugs of the Mideast. Some of these experiments have been destructive and premature, while others have added new dimensions of experience for the venturesome. In the long run, transculturation and mutual appreciation of contributions seem to be the only methods that will permanently ease cultural conflicts. Most people, however, are far from recognizing that cultures can work into each other rather than clash or dominate.

SUMMARY

The cultures of the world vary widely and vary with respect to the four components of tools, products, symbols, and rules. Technologies, or systems of tools, vary in the energy that they capture from the low level of a man swinging a stone axe to the high level of a nuclear power plant. Some technologies are based on tools and others on machines. Products, or systems of goods and services, can display variety or simplicity, different degrees of standardization, and different comparisons of items concerned with food, clothing, and shelter. Symbols, or systems of communication, can be specialized or unspecialized. Rules, or systems of role definitions, can embody many different standards of judgment. For example, people can be judged fit to perform roles because they have performed at a certain level of achievement, or they can be judged fit because they come from a certain family, have a certain skin color, or display some other quality unrelated to achievement. No component of culture is uniquely determined by any other component.

Cultural conflict arises when there is active disagreement among human beings or groups of people over tools, symbols, products, and rules. These conflicts are summarized in clashing definitions of the role of human being. In the twentieth century, racism, assimilation, separatism, revolutionism, and reverse racism have been strategies of conflict and conflict solving. The strategy of transculturation, based on a synthesis of cultures, has not been extensively tried, but is in the stage of experiment in some youth movements.

Notes

[1] Charles F. Marden and Gladys Meyer, *Minorities in American Society* (New York: American Book Company, 1968), p. 64.

[2] Marden and Meyer, *Minorities*, p. 35.

[3] Gunnar Myrdal, *An American Dilemma* (New York: Harper & Row, Publishers, 1944).

[4] Brewton Berry, *Race and Ethnic Relations* (Boston: Houghton Mifflin Company, 1958), p. 157.

Suggested Readings

Bird, C. *Born Female: The High Cost of Keeping Women Down*, New York: David McKay Co., Inc., 1968.

Deloria, Jr., V. *Custer Died for Your Sins: An Indian Manifesto*, London: Collier-Macmillan Ltd., 1969.

Friedan, B. *The Feminine Mystique*, New York: Dell Publishing Co., Inc., 1965 (paper).

Glazer, N. and Moynihan, D. P. *Beyond the Melting Pot: The Negroes, Puerto Ricans, Jews, Italians and Irish of New York City*, Cambridge: M.I.T. Press, 1963 (paper).

Killiam, L. M. *The Impossible Revolution: Black Power and the American Dream*, New York: Random House, Inc., 1968 (paper).

Liebow, E. *Tally's Corner*, Boston: Little, Brown and Company, 1967 (paper).

Murdock, G. P. *Social Structure*, Glencoe: The Free Press, 1965 (paper).

Myrdal, G. *et al., An American Dilemma: The Negro Problem and Modern Democracy*, two volumes, 20th anniversary edition, New York: Harper & Row, Publishers, 1962 (paper).

Northrop, F. S. *The Meeting of East and West*, New York: The Macmillan Company, 1960 (paper).

Reich, C. A. *The Greening of America*, New York: Random House, Inc., 1970.

Roszak, T. *The Making of a Counter Culture: Reflections on the Technocratic Society and Its Youthful Opposition*, Garden City: Doubleday & Company, Inc., 1969 (paper).

CHAPTER FOUR: SOCIAL ORGANIZATION

Previous chapters have traced the progression of human development from the impulsive infant to the child who takes the role of particular others ("What would my mother say if I did this?") to the child who takes the role of others in specific positions ("What would a teacher say if I did this?") to the person who takes the role of the generalized other, or human being ("What would people say if I did this?"). Beyond the role of human being is the person as creative role-maker, or "I." Generally, the social sciences are descriptions of dialogues between the claims of the social self ("me") and the creative self ("I").

Anthropologists make a special contribution to the social sciences by taking the role of the other in different cultures. They extend the vision and range of alternatives for human beings by asking, "What would the Eskimo, or people in some other cultural group, say if someone did this?" They show that the role of human being varies from one culture to the next and that different cultures are founded on different postulates. Students of cultural conflict make a special application of the anthropologist's contribution. They show that in a situation where one group is dominant over another, the stronger group is likely to make two roles of human being, one for its own members and one for the members of the weaker group. The acceptance and/or rejection of the split role of human being by members of the stronger and weaker groups forms the background for cultural conflict.

In concrete situations where people meet one another face to face, it is almost never the case that they govern their behaviors fully in agreement with cultural definitions of role. For example, when someone takes a new job he is usually informed of the rights and duties attached to the position and of the meaning of his function in a larger context. A secretary may be told that she is only supposed to take dictation from certain people and that she should not provide junior executives with extra office supplies. At the beginning she is likely to follow the rules rigidly because she only has the official definition of role to guide her. However, in a short time she will notice that many people around her do not approve of her actions. She will find out that while the personnel manager believes that secretaries should not provide extra office supplies to junior executives, other secretaries give away such supplies frequently and the junior executives expect them to do so. She will also observe that secretaries who give away office supplies and take dictation for anyone who needs it are rewarded with gifts and courtesy, while those who follow the official role are ridiculed. Finally, she will notice that the other secretaries are not very friendly to her and talk about how she has disrupted a happy office.

Normally, the secretary will take action on such information by adjusting her role definition. She will take the role of particular others and ask, "What would this particular junior executive think if I did this?" She will find that some junior executives expect special dictation services, others expect extra office supplies, and others play by the official rules. When she takes the role of particular others, she does so only in the context of the official and cultural definitions of role. She takes the role of a particular junior executive, not of a particular person. Once the secretary has figured out what the particular others want her to do in the context of her official role, she devises a role definition of a secretary in her particular office. This role definition includes the actions she is expected to do in the office. These actions may or may not differ widely from those prescribed in the official role. However, regardless of their differing from the official set of rights and duties, these expectations are of the greatest importance to the secretary. In the concrete social situation, role defined as expected behavior is the most significant factor.

The importance of role as expectation can be shown through striking examples. Sometimes when workers are dissatisfied with job conditions and cannot strike because of a clause in their contract, they will "work by rule." This tactic involves performing only those specific tasks written into the job descriptions and demanding all the rights spelled out in the rule book. In any complex work situation, work by rule will bring the entire operation to a halt because performance of task depends upon informal expectations of those involved in the task. For example, workers in airport control towers have caused long delays in takeoffs and landings when they have insisted on following all the rules.

Even more critical is the situation of a military unit in wartime. On the battlefield many decisions must be made that are not covered by the regulations, or actually deviate from the regulations, if the unit is to survive and gain its objective. Along with any *formal organization* officially specifying rights and duties for each position goes an *informal organization* based on concrete expectations of participants.

The term *expectations* can be taken in two ways, both of which are important in the study of social organization. People may say that a politician is expected to keep his campaign promises. By this they mean that politicians have a moral obligation to keep their campaign promises, or that they should keep them. The same people may say that they do not expect politicians to keep their campaign promises. Here they mean that it is safe to predict that politicians will not keep their campaign promises. In the study of social organization we are primarily concerned with the predictive use of expectations. Unless people have some reliable anticipation of what those around them will do in various situations, there can be no social relations and organization. Characters who do not understand this rule have interested novelists and playwrights for centuries. Perhaps the most famous example of a character insensitive to role expectations is Cervantes' Don Quixote, who attempted to follow the Medieval code of chivalry in an age of self-interest and rising commercialism. To dream the impossible dream is in most cases to disrupt the normal expectations of others. Often the use of expectations as moral obligations and the use of expectations as predictions of behavior get confused. This is because people count on their predictions to be correct when they plan their own activities. When the other acts differently from expectations, people are frustrated in carrying out their plans and tend to blame the other for their failure. In this way an expectation that was merely a prediction becomes a rule with praise and blame attached. Because the other did not act according to the prediction, the frustrated person will say, "He should have acted as I expected."

Social organization is the study of cultural roles in action, or roles as expected behaviors. Society is a process which works by people taking the roles of particular others in cultural contexts and thereby forming generalized expectations of behavior. Viewing roles as sets of expected behaviors around a task or function allows one to account for informal organizations flourishing within formal definitions of rights and duties, and for the predictions and anticipations underlying the conduct of everyday life.

ROLE NETWORKS AND INSTITUTIONS

The political scientist Heinz Eulau has pointed out: "If a relationship had to be defined anew with each interaction, or if expectations had to be elaborated with every new encounter, stable social life would be impossible."[1] Roles are never found in isolation. They are always found in networks clustered around the major social functions and processes like economics (the creation, preservation, destruction, and distribution of culture), politics (the ordering of human activities with respect to one another), education (the transmission of information about culture), and appreciation (the use and enjoyment of culture). In this sense, roles are sets of expectations concerning the performance of parts of major social processes and functions. The role networks clustered around social processes form institutions, or the ways in which social functions are carried out. Thus, there are economic, political, educational, and appreciative institutions in cultural groups.

Within any institution there may be a number of formal organizations, or role networks, devised to carry out particular purposes relating to the performance of the major social function. For example, in carrying out the function of economics there are business firms, labor unions, and government agencies, all of which are part of the economic institution. Just as major debates take place over role definitions, significant conflicts occur over the purposes that should be served by role networks, or organizations. Should a business firm aim primarily at making a profit, providing high quality goods, or performing social services like hiring the hard-core unemployed? Debates like this occur about every organization in contemporary Western societies. Organizations can be described according to the purposes they actually serve, the purposes that people believe they serve, and the purposes that people believe they should serve. These three descriptions of purpose can widely separate as in the case of a business firm which seeks growth and stability and whose stockholders believe that it seeks social service and that it should aim at making a maximum profit.

Role networks usually have a central role that is defined generally and vaguely. Eulau remarks that in most cases "a role is at the core of several other roles, making for a network of roles that can be very complex." He continues that the central role does not have clearly defined expectations and that only minimum agreement on it is likely to exist. The roles of politician in the political process, teacher in the educational process, worker in the economic process, and consumer (user of goods) in the appreciative process are examples of such general roles at the center of role networks. Eulau observes that it is difficult to say what behavior is expected of the politician without first inquiring. At the center of all social roles is the role of human being which is the most indefinitely defined of all.

The most interesting social roles are those unthinkable in the absence of another role. There could be no representative without a voter, no parent without a child, no husband without a wife, no leader without a follower, no teacher without a student, and no doctor without a patient. In these cases the very definition of the role includes another role. The study of such roles forms a large part of investigation into social organization. They are often the key relations to consider in describing how a social function is performed. Roles that are unthinkable in the absence of other roles also show that taking the role of the other is an important process. The representative can understand what he is expected to do only by judging his actions in relation to the role of the voter.

WHY ROLES ARE PERFORMED

Social relations can be placed on a range running from those in which people take the roles of particular others to those in which people take the roles of functionaries or generalized others. For example, in close friendship relations, marital relations, and other family relations, it is likely that people will ask, "What would some particular other think if I did this?" For example, a child would ask, "What would my mother think?" On the contrary, when one is performing such actions as driving a car, he is likely to ask, "What would some general other, in this case another driver or a pedestrian, do and think if I did this?" Thus, social relations can range from the personal to the impersonal. Most social relations are neither completely personal nor fully impersonal. A mother is usually conscious of what she is generally expected to do as a mother, as well as what she is expected to do as the mother of a particular child. A worker is usually conscious of what he is expected to do as the colleague of other particular workers, as well as what he is generally expected to do as an occupant of his formal position. Large-scale organizations are generally judged to breed more impersonal relations than small groups. While this is correct, it is important to remember that informal organizations grow up in most formal organizations. These informal organizations are relatively personal and they may sway the formal organization from its official goal, as when workers slow down output. Or they may aid the formal organization in more efficiently realizing its goal, as when workers cut through red tape to get the job accomplished. It is not a good general rule to state that personal relations are always more satisfying than impersonal relations. Sometimes a person would rather be judged according to his achievement in performing a function rather than as a particular individual.

Whether relations tend to be personal or impersonal in a particular situation, there must be some way of making sure that enough expectations are satisfied to allow the carrying on of social processes. There are a number of ways in which going along with expectations is enforced in social situations. The means to insure compliance with expectations vary from force to persuasion, with many steps along the way. Political scientist Harold Lasswell has presented a useful classification of the ways in which human behavior is controlled. Lasswell observes that the means of enforcing compliance with expectations can be divided into symbols, violence, goods, and practices. This is similar to the classification of the major kinds of culture into symbols, tools, products, and rules.

Control by *symbols* works by convincing the person that he should comply with the expectations associated with his role. There are several varieties of symbolic control. The person may be ridiculed for failing to comply with expectations, he may be threatened, he may be told that it is his duty to fulfill expectations, he may be persuaded that it is in his interest to fulfill expectations, and he may be deceived about the consequences of fulfilling expectations. Praise and blame are given through symbols and are very powerful techniques of social control. It is often possible to get a person to perform an action simply by smiling or frowning.

Control by *violence* works by using those tools known as weapons to enforce behavior. While praise and blame are techniques of control used throughout social life, violence is usually restricted to cases in which important rules are broken, or in which accomplishing plans important to people is at stake.

Control by *goods* works by using products to gain compliance with expectations. If control by symbols is associated with praise and blame, control by goods is associated with rewards and punishments. Here the person is induced to comply with expectations either by the offer of a product that he desires or by the withdrawal of a product that he expects to have. Many people equate control by violence with control by goods, but there are important distinctions. The clear case of violence is the use of force to remove a human being physically from a certain place. The clear case of using goods to secure compliance is the bribe offered someone if he does not do or does do some action. There is a difference between being deprived of movement and being offered an opportunity.

THERE ARE FOUR METHODS OF SOCIAL CONTROL

Control by *practices* works by using rules to make a person go along with expectations. For example, if there is a general and informal expectation that professors will hold their classes in specific rooms, and enough professors do not fulfill this expectation, the university administration may draw up a rule requiring that classes be held in the rooms specified on the schedule sheet. Some professors may be persuaded to hold their classes in the specified rooms simply because a rule has been passed, but most likely the rule will contain penalties in case someone breaks it.

The various means of social control have two aspects. First, they are used to insure that human beings fulfill enough of their role expectations to allow the performance of key social functions. Here they function to secure the integration or harmonization of social life. Second, they are used to maintain the dominance of some groups over others in social life. Here they function to secure the maintenance of a stratification system. Social organization can be considered a linking together of role networks in the performance of social function, or the arrangement of role networks in relations of dominance and subordination. We turn now to the second aspect, stratification.

SOCIAL STRATIFICATION

When role networks are arranged on a scale of rich-poor, honored-dishonored, or dominant-subordinate the problem of *social stratification* becomes primary. In premodern societies, social stratification is closely tied to the performance of functions. In some cases, there is a clear arrangement of the major social functions into a hierarchy, or ladder, of wealth, respect, and power. People performing the functions on top of the ladder have the most products, honor, and control over decisions affecting themselves, and others. Those performing functions on the bottom of the ladder have the least of these desired things. In most modern societies there is no clear arrangement of social functions into a single hierarchy or ladder. For example, clergymen may gain more respect than popular singing stars, but the singers may have more wealth than the clergymen. Political bosses may have more power in making decisions than either clergymen or singing stars, but less wealth than the singing stars and less respect than the clergymen. Thus, in modern societies the stratification system is more independent of the performance of social function than it is in many premodern societies.

One of the earliest descriptions of a stratification system was provided by the ancient Greek philosopher Plato. In his *Republic* Plato described a stratification system in which the position of a group on the social ladder corresponded to the network of roles performed by its members. There were three classes in Plato's scheme. The guardians, who were on top of the social ladder, performed the function of coordinating the performances of all other roles and making sure that important tasks were accomplished without disagreements. Plato gave them the highest honor and the most power, but believed that they would not desire wealth. In Plato's scheme, the guardians would be philosopher-kings who would rule for the good of the whole and prize thought over action. He held that some group had to perform the function of making roles fit together with minimum conflict, and that any group other than philosopher-kings would rule in the self-interest of its members. Plato's second class was composed of warriors, who occupied the middle of the social ladder. The function of the warriors was to defend the community against external attack and to carry out the decisions of the guardians. The third class was composed of workers and specialists, who occupied the lowest rung of the social ladder. They provided the goods and services for continuing human existence. The workers were directed and protected by the warriors and coordinated by the guardians. Plato's stratification system was his sketch of an ideal society. There has never been a society in which philosopher-kings, chosen by merit, have ruled. Plato himself realized how difficult it would be to establish such a society. He wrote that the guardians could only rule if they convinced the others that the guardians were a special race made of gold, the warriors were another race made of silver, and the workers were another race made of bronze. This "noble lie" has been seen as a grave defect in Plato's thought by many thinkers, although every ruling group has used such a "lie" to defend its dominant position.

Although it is a description of an ideal, and not an account of any real society, Plato's system of stratification has had a great effect on Western thought. The philosopher Alfred North Whitehead has remarked that Western thought is a series of "footnotes to Plato." Plato is important here because he shows that social function and social stratification are closely related. In traditional India there was an actual system of social stratification that closely resembled Plato's scheme and included social functions similar to those outlined by Plato. The Indian caste system is a supreme example of a stratification system that orders social function into a hierarchy.

A caste system of stratification is one in which people are assigned as a result of birth to perform the various social roles. Plato did not have a caste system because his guardians, warriors, and workers were assigned to their tasks according to ability rather than family. In traditional India there were five major groups. The highest caste was composed of Brahmins, or priests and religious leaders. The second caste was composed of warriors, princes, and administrators. The third and fourth castes were composed of peasants, merchants, craftsmen, and unskilled workers. The four castes correspond roughly to Plato's classes, with the Brahmans approximating the philosopher-kings, the princes approximating the warriors, and the two other castes corresponding to the workers. The fifth group was composed of people outside the caste system, or untouchables. The untouchables were sweepers, who performed the function of sanitation. An elaborate code of rules forbade contact between them and members of the four other castes. The existence of the untouchables in the Indian caste system and not in Plato's class system can be explained partly by the fact that the Indian system was religiously based, while Plato's scheme was based on looking directly at patterns of social life. In the Hindu beliefs that underlay the caste system, human waste material was accorded certain magical properties. Possession of a person's waste material was thought in some areas to allow control over the person's fate. Thus, those who handled this material were given a subhuman position. In Plato's system there was no magic and, therefore, no need for untouchables.

Even in India, the caste system was never as simple as the preceding description would have it. There were more than five thousand subcastes and their composition and functions changed continuously. The historical movement throughout the world has been away from an overlap between stratification and social function and in the direction of much more complex relations. As cultures have come into greater contact and cultural objects like tools, symbols, rules, and products have become more specialized, social thinkers have made many ambitious attempts to describe the social ladder. One of the most influential views of stratification was developed by Karl Marx. Marx held that the basis for determining the social ladder was ownership and control of tools. In a famous passage in *The Communist Manifesto*, Marx and Friedrich Engels commented that the history of society has been the history of class struggles between those who have owned the tools necessary to manufacture goods and other tools, and those who have sold their labor to the owners or who have actually been owned as slaves: "Freeman and slave, patrician and plebeian, lord and serf, guildmaster and journeyman, in a word, oppressor and oppressed, stood in constant opposition to one another, carried on . . . a fight that each time ended, either in a revolutionary reconstitution of society at large, or in the common ruin of the contending classes."[2]

For Marx and Engels all social divisions could be explained on the basis of ownership and control of the means of production. With respect to rules, Marx and Engels held that the state is the "executive committee" of the class owning the tools. Laws reflect the interest of owners in maintaining and expanding their holdings of property. With regard to symbols, Marx and Engels held that ideas stem from the relations of various groups to the ownership of tools. In a striking passage they ask, "Does it require deep intuition to comprehend that man's ideas, views, and conceptions, in one word, man's consciousness, changes with every change in the conditions of his material existence, in his social relations and in his social life?"[3] For example, the factory worker who becomes a shopkeeper will frequently change his ideas on the need for strong labor unions. With reference to products, Marx and Engels point out that the owners gain the most wealth and are able to live in comparative luxury at the expense of other groups.

THREE SYSTEMS OF STRATIFICATION

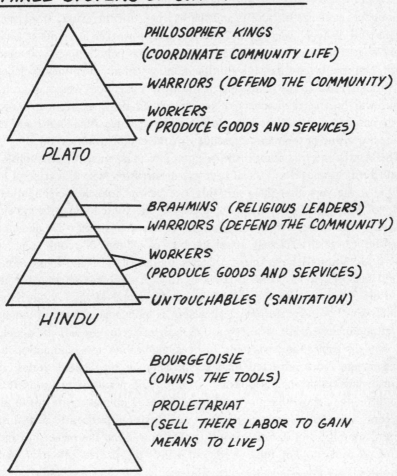

PLATO

- PHILOSOPHER KINGS (COORDINATE COMMUNITY LIFE)
- WARRIORS (DEFEND THE COMMUNITY)
- WORKERS (PRODUCE GOODS AND SERVICES)

HINDU

- BRAHMINS (RELIGIOUS LEADERS)
- WARRIORS (DEFEND THE COMMUNITY)
- WORKERS (PRODUCE GOODS AND SERVICES)
- UNTOUCHABLES (SANITATION)

MARX

- BOURGEOISIE (OWNS THE TOOLS)
- PROLETARIAT (SELL THEIR LABOR TO GAIN MEANS TO LIVE)

The classes described by Marx and Engels are not like Hindu castes because one does not have to be born into them. They become like castes when, through inheritance, owners pass property on to their children. The Marxist interpretation of class and stratification is widely held outside of the United States and is held within the United States by radical groups such as the Black

Panthers and the Students for a Democratic Society. In describing contemporary societies, Marxists say that there are two central roles around which all other roles are organized. The role of bourgeois is the role of owner of productive tools. The role of proletarian is the role of the worker who owns no productive property and who must sell his labor to survive. The owner attempts to maximize his profits and thereby prevents the worker from gaining the full share of what he has produced. The worker attempts to gain higher wages, but is at a disadvantage because he has only his body and mind to sell. Marxists believe that the stratification system in present-day societies is being simplified to the point that in the West tremendous masses of proletarians will face small numbers of owners. When the lines become drawn clearly enough, there will be a revolutionary struggle resulting in the end of private ownership of tools and, consequently, the end of stratification.

The Marxist interpretation is the beginning of most current discussions of social stratification. Present social scientists depart from Marx and attempt to show how the view that there are only two central roles is oversimplified. Critics of Marx point out that in countries like the United States the system of stratification is becoming more complex rather than simpler. Tremendous organizations which decisively affect the lives of millions of people, such as universities, hospitals, government agencies, military forces, and foundations are not managed for a profit. Control of tools has become separated from ownership of them. Do the stockholders of General Motors control the assembly line? Workers do not face owners as individuals. Powerful unions face strong managements. Those who are most respected are not the people who own the tools. Supreme Court Justices, medical doctors, and university professors are more respected than businessmen in the United States, as shown by surveys in which people are asked to rank various occupations. It is more difficult to show that the most powerful decision makers are not those who control the tools. However, governmental decisions frequently go against business interests, and it is safe to state that power and the ownership and control of tools do not fully overlap. Finally, the people who own and control tools are not always the ones who use the widest variety and greatest number of products. Celebrities, like movie stars, are the consumption leaders who use the newest and widest variety of products. They do not usually own or control the tools with which these goods were produced.

The many problems in the Marxist view of stratification have led social scientists to state that there are at least three separate, though interrelated, stratification systems in contemporary societies. This idea was spelled out by the sociologist Max Weber. Weber held that the three primary bases for ranking people are class, status, and power. For Weber, class is defined according to income and economic interest. Inequalities of income set various groups off from one another in terms of the kinds of lives that are led within them. For example, poor people cannot afford the same range of products as members of the middle class and, therefore, lead different kinds of lives on the whole. Status is defined as the ranking of various life styles on the basis of prestige. It is not always the case that those who can afford the most products are also those who gain the most prestige. The newly rich family, throwing its money around and not acting according to etiquette, is scorned rather than respected. As time goes on it is likely that such a family will learn how to behave according to the codes associated with high status and will gain respect. Thus, status follows class and the two frequently do not overlap. The third area of stratification is power, which Weber defines as "the chance of a man or a number of men to realize their own will in a communal action even against the resistance of others who are participating in the action."[4] Power can be exerted by governmental officials, political bosses, and managers of organizations who have neither very great wealth nor very high status. Thus, in contemporary Western societies, stratification has been broken up into several systems.

Not only are there several social ladders in current societies, but it is also difficult to identify where a person stands on each ladder. Some sociologists have attempted to get a general ranking of people by combining considerations of income, educational level, occupation, race, and residence. They have shown that white professional men with high income, who live in urban areas, rank higher than other Americans. However, when it comes to more specific judgments there are great difficulties. While it would seem easy to rank people according to economic class, even here there are difficulties of considering how to weigh fringe benefits, expense accounts, special services, and the general physical environment. More problems appear with respect to status and power. These two measures of rank appear to vary according to specific situations. Thus, some groups accord great respect to military officers, while other groups scorn them. Some groups honor clergymen and others do not. Respect for farmers varies widely. The same holds true for power. Depending upon the area in which the decision is made, different people and groups will have power. Military officers may have much power in determining what kind of weapons will be used and how they will be used in a battlefield situation. However, they are likely to have much less power in determining what will be taught at a college or university. This point has been shown by the success that the American military services have had in gaining certain weapons and using them on the battlefield, and the failure they have experienced in maintaining ROTC courses on many campuses. On the other hand, college faculties have demonstrated power over the content of curriculum, but very little power over determining what weapons systems will be designed, constructed, and used. Who has the status and power in contemporary Western societies depends in large degree on the issues and areas that one finds important. Modern societies become increasingly complex in their stratification systems. One mark of our present age is the rapid expansion of the number of roles available to people. Putting these roles into a single scheme of ranking like Plato developed and Marx attempted to develop is a problem as yet unresolved by contemporary social scientists.

WHO'S ON TOP ?

One way of making sense out of the maze of different rankings in current American society is to focus on the place of specialization. While anthropologists have described the variety of cultures around the world, sociologists have described the variety of roles present in contemporary cultures. The more tasks become defined as specialities, the more such considerations as control of working conditions, independence of judgment on the job, and possession of special symbols and knowledge become important factors in determining status. Perhaps the emerging social ladder is one on which people are ranked according to their possession of specialized skills and positions in large organizations.

SOCIAL MOBILITY

Traditionally, Americans have believed that if a person worked hard enough and took advantage of the opportunities presented to him, he could rise from a low position on the social ladder to a higher one, or at least pave the way for his children to rise. While there is some mobility, or movement up and down the various social scales, in every society, both mobility within a person's lifetime and mobility over more than one generation have been exaggerated in American folklore. The sociologists Seymour M. Lipset and Reinhard Bendix point out that the stratification system in the United States is so complex that the very concept of social mobility is difficult to define: "Men may change their position in the social structure in many ways; but we do not know which ways are most significant to their sense of improvement or decline."[5] However, certain statements can be made with a high degree of confidence. Until quite recently black Americans were subjected to a caste-like situation in which their skin color hampered them from gaining the employment opportunities of whites. Women also have been barred from occupational improvement, and sociologist P. Sorokin even suggested that they are treated as a separate class. Americans living in poverty ridden backgrounds have often lacked the early childhood training necessary to the desire to achieve in contemporary society. In a world in which the possession of specialized skills is increasingly necessary for advancement, any barriers to achievement in learning are barriers to upward social mobility.

SUMMARY

Social organization is the study of how role networks are related in such a way that the major social processes—economics, politics, appreciation, and education—are performed, and how role networks are arranged on a scale or hierarchy. In general, role networks are related to one another through the act of taking the role of the other. In personal relations, people take the roles of particular others by asking, "What would this person do and think if I did this?" In impersonal relations, people take the roles of more generalized others by asking, "What would a person in this position do and think if I did this?" Both personal and impersonal relations involve expected behaviors which enable people to carry out their plans with some confidence about the outcomes. These expectations are enforced by a variety of means including violence, persuasion, rule making, and economic rewards and punishments.

Role networks are arranged in hierarchies or scales. In premodern societies, roles involved in the performance of the major social functions are arranged in a one-dimensional hierarchy. In modern societies the hierarchies become multi-dimensional; there are many ladders rather than only one, and the ladders crisscross one another. Current sociologists have singled out class, status, and power as the most important bases for stratification, but it is difficult to determine who has the most status and power. At present, hierarchies of skill seem to be particularly important.

Notes

[1] Heinz Eulau, *The Behavioral Persuasion in Politics* (New York: Random House, Inc., 1963), p. 43.

[2] Karl Marx and Friedrich Engels, *The Communist Manifesto* (New York: Appleton-Century-Crofts, 1955), p. 9.

[3] Marx and Engels, *The Communist Manifesto*, pp. 29-30.

[4] Hans Gerth and C. Wright Mills, *From Max Weber* (New York: Oxford University Press, 1946), p. 180.

[5] Seymour Martin Lipset and Reinhard Bendix, *Social Mobility in Industrial Society* (Berkeley: University of California Press, 1966), p. 112.

Suggested Readings

Berger, P. L. *Invitation to Sociology: A Humanistic Perspective*, Garden City: Doubleday & Company, Inc., 1963 (paper).

Bottomore, T. H. *Classes in Modern Society*, New York: Random House, Inc., 1968 (paper).

Chinoy, E. *Sociological Perspectives*, second ed., New York: Random House, Inc., 1968 (paper).

Lipset, S. M. and Bendix, R. *Social Mobility in Industrial Society*, Berkeley: University of California Press, 1966 (paper).

Marcuse, H. *One Dimensional Man*, Boston: Beacon Press, 1964 (paper).

Marshall, T. H. *Class, Citizenship, and Social Development*, Garden City: Doubleday & Company, Inc., 1965 (paper).

Mayer, K. B. and Buckley, W. *Class and Society*, New York: Random House, Inc., 1968 (paper).

Mills, C. W. *The Sociological Imagination*, New York: Oxford University Press, 1967 (paper).

Veblen, T. *The Theory of the Leisure Class*, New York: New American Library of World Literature, Inc., 1954 (paper).

CHAPTER FIVE: ECONOMIC ROLES

The study of *economics* treats those social processes involved with the creation, preservation, destruction, and distribution of cultural objects. Houses are built, repaired, wrecked, bought, and sold. Economists study such processes. The study of economics describes the ways in which resources are assigned or distributed to the various realms of culture. It is centrally concerned with the part of culture defined by tools. Are high-rise apartments or garden apartments built? Are they built with advanced tools or traditional tools?

Economists have traditionally begun their investigations with an emphasis on the importance of scarcity in human affairs. For the economist, human beings are in a situation in which they cannot satisfy their needs and wants, or realize their possibilities, without working to change natural resources into products with the use of tools. People cannot survive without food, clothing, and shelter. Once human beings become producers, or toolmakers and tool-users, the problem arises of how various resources are to be apportioned, or distributed, to the creation of different products, and how these products are to be distributed. Which houses should be built, who will get them, how many of them will there be? This problem can be looked at in two ways. First, one can ask, "How are resources actually allocated, or assigned, and products distributed?" (Who actually gets the houses?) Second, one can ask, "How should resources be allocated and products distributed?" (Who should be getting the houses?) The first question forms the basis of empirical economics. *Empirical economics* describes the ways in which scarce resources are allocated, or apportioned, to various human activities. The second question forms the basis of normative economics. *Normative economics* discusses and evaluates the various principles for determining the ways in which scarce resources should be allocated to various human activities and cultural objects.

The condition of scarcity in human affairs has a wide variety of clashing meanings. For some economists it means that people must work to satisfy their most basic needs. While the list of things that people need varies from one thinker to the next, it is clear that some physical and mental effort is necessary to provide such goods as food, clothing, and shelter. Beyond such physical needs, there is no clear agreement about the necessities of human existence. In our contemporary world, many products are manufactured which have little relation to the satisfaction of physical needs. For example, stereo tape decks, underground newspapers, and electric guitars are not necessary for physical survival. This has led economists to say that if they are concerned with the ways in which resources are allocated to the various human activities, they cannot base their study on a restricted list of needs. Thus, in the modern world, they have tended to base scarcity on wants rather than needs.

Even if a person has the food, clothing, and shelter necessary to maintain his existence, he still may *want* other objects or food, clothing, and shelter in greater quality and quantity. When there is no scarcity in relation to physical survival, there still may be scarcity with respect to the satisfaction of desires, or wants. Many people who cannot afford them want sport cars, fashionable clothes, and expensive liquor. The importance of want led economists in the nineteenth century to consider the allocation of resources to the satisfaction of various wants. They stated that the quest for want satisfaction was powered by the desire for pleasure or happiness, supposedly universal in human beings. Thus, products could be compared according to the amounts of pleasure or happiness that they gave to individuals. Along with the notion of pleasure as the dominant force in behavior came the assumption that human wants were endless and could not be satisfied by any system of producing and distributing goods and services. The idea was that people could never be satisfied, whatever they had. Economics became the study of how human beings, seeking pleasure, competed for goods and services.

Economists in the twentieth century have questioned the assumptions of nineteenth-century economists. They have shown that it is difficult to argue that human beings always seek maximum pleasure or happiness, unless pleasure and happiness are defined so generally as to mean that human beings prefer what they prefer. Some people will forego a good meal to visit a sick friend, even if the meal would be more pleasant. This cannot be explained by the pleasure principle. Contemporary economists have also believed that even if people do always seek pleasure, it is impossible to compare the satisfactions gained by different human beings, or even the same human being at different times, because pleasure is a feeling not observable by anyone else but the person experiencing it at a certain time. Along with their criticism of the pleasure principle, economists have also criticized the idea that human wants are infinite and cannot be satisfied by any system of producing and distributing goods and services. It is possible for people to be relatively satisfied with the goods and services they have received and to demand little or anything more than what they have. Even salesmen have an idea of the number of sales which will satisfy them and tend not to exceed this number. Some sales managers who deplore this fact call the level of satisfaction the "comfort zone."

A big factor in determining the level of wants is the general expectation of the social self, or "me." If the role of human being in a certain culture defines a person as one who has limitless wants, people in that culture are likely to display a high level of wants. If the role of human being in a culture defines a person as one who is satisfied when his physical needs are met, people in that culture are likely to display a low level of wants. The existence of widespread advertising in the Western world, continuously attempting to start wants, is one indication that having limitless wants is not a universal condition of human nature.

The fact that economists have criticized the pleasure principle, and the idea that human beings have limitless wants does not mean that they have given up the idea of scarcity. While people do not inevitably desire more and more, they do have a wide variety of preferences and do see choices in plans for the future. One built-in limitation of the human condition is that only certain projects are possible within the limitations of space and time. There cannot be two tallest buildings in the same city. Out of all the possible uses of resources that human beings can imagine, some projects will be chosen and other projects will be rejected. Thus, even if needs can be satisfied and wants are not limitless, scarcity may still be present if there are limited means for satisfying preferences. It is not built into the human condition that people must have different scales of preference and seek commitment of resources to incompatible projects (not everyone wants to own the tallest building in the city), but such problems do face people in contemporary Western societies.

ECONOMIC MAN

In the past, economists have worked with a role of the human being known as economic man. This role is a *model*, and no actual human being ever lived up to its standards. It has been used to show what the world would be like if everyone attempted to satisfy his personal desires with perfect efficiency. A symbol of Western culture in the nineteenth century, the notion of economic man has come increasingly under attack in the twentieth century. The idea of economic man has been important in the general historical development of the West, as well as to the study of economics.

Economic man is defined as an individual with a number of preferences, who can put these preferences on a scale in such a way that they form a consistent ranking. For example, a person with only three preferences, a, b, and c, would be able to say that if he preferred a to b and b to c, he would also prefer a to c. For example, a person who preferred gin to bourbon and bourbon to Scotch would also prefer gin to Scotch. Therefore, economic man knows all of his preferences and also knows how to rank them consistently. Further, economic man has knowledge of the probabilities that he will satisfy his various preferences. He would know what chance he had to get a fifth of gin. He also has knowledge of the alternative means through which his preferences can be realized and can choose the ones that cost him the least in terms of preferences sacrificed. If a fifth of gin cost twenty dollars and a fifth of Scotch cost two dollars, he might decide to buy the Scotch. Herbert Simon has remarked that economic man "selects the best alternative from among all those available to him."[1] This is the definition of *efficiency*. Economic man is, finally, given the ability to see the world clearly. His judgments are distorted neither by prejudice nor emotion. He would not pretend that gin cost one dollar when it really cost twenty dollars. Simon notes that economic man "deals with the 'real world' in all its complexity."[2] Economic man acts, in all cases, to maximize the satisfaction of his preferences. Economists call economic man rational, and the definition of economic man agrees with the definition of economic rationality.

ECONOMIC MAN AND NORMAL MAN

As a description of the way in which human beings actually behave, the description of economic man is very inaccurate. Hardly anyone is fully aware of all of his preferences, much less is he able to rank them into a consistent order. Further, nobody knows the probabilities that various preferences will be satisfied, nor all of the alternative means through which they can be satisfied. Thus, nobody can select the best alternative from among all available alternatives. Finally, nobody ever fully knows the real world, undistorted by prejudice and emotion. Simon observes that the views of the world which people have are "drastically simplified" models of "the buzzing, blooming confusion that constitutes the real world."[3]

These criticisms of economic man, though very important, are not as important as the point that people will tend to come close to or attempt to come close to the behavior of economic man only if they accept the role of economic man as a truthful definition of the role of human being. If people take the role of economic man when they ask, "What will people think if I do this?" they will strive to act according to the principles of economic rationality. During the nineteenth century, many people, particularly businessmen, accepted the role of economic man as the role of human being, at least in their business dealings. Acceptance of this role has become less ready in the twentieth century with the rise of vast concentrations of political power and recognition that human behavior is largely patterned by basic cultural postulates. Greater knowledge of cultures throughout the world has shown Western economists that the notion of economic man is tied up closely with various European religious, political and legal traditions. Economists use the idea of economic man to show what would happen if people behaved according to the principles of economic rationality. Thus, the notion of economic man is a model. They agree that human behavior is far from meeting these principles, but believe that in situations where people come close to living the role of economic man, this notion is a useful tool for describing and predicting human activity.

BUSINESS ORGANIZATIONS AND INSTITUTIONS

The specialized roles that actually characterize the economic process of creating, preserving, destroying, and distributing cultural objects are far more complex than the role of economic man. In the actual economies of today, large business corporations, labor unions, and government agencies on many levels determine the allocation of resources to various uses. In each organization there is an interlocking and complex set of formal roles tied to fulfilling the declared purpose of the organization. There is also a web of informal relations, reshaping organizational purposes or supporting the fulfillment of those purposes. Understanding of the roles making up the economic process in a contemporary economy demands more than just a description of economic rationality.

The business firm has been the central institution and organization in Western economies. In capitalist economies, the *business firm* has had the traditional purpose of supplying goods and services for a maximum profit. Historically, the business firm has developed from a proprietorship or partnership to a corporation. In the *proprietorship* or *partnership*, the owner or owners of the business firm are responsible for the losses caused by the firm.

THE STOCKHOLDER AND THE PROPRIETOR

They assume unlimited liability for the debts of the firm and the consequences of its actions. In a sense, the firm is identified with the proprietor or the partners. The business *corporation* is one of the major social inventions in world history. Having its roots in Roman law, the corporation is a legal, or fictive, person. The stockholders, people who own it, are neither responsible for the losses caused by it nor the results of its actions. They have an opportunity, however, to share in its profits. The corporation can be sued and can bring legal actions, it can be taxed and it can be declared bankrupt, or unable to meet its financial obligations. When the bankruptcy of a corporation occurs, the stockholders do not have to pay the debts, as in a proprietorship or a partnership. Similarly, when a corporation loses a court case, the stockholders do not go to jail or pay the fine or judgment.

The corporation caused two important developments in modern history. First, by creating a way in which a large number of people could participate in financing expensive and complex ventures, the corporations became a means of unprecedented commercial and industrial development. Many people could combine their resources in projects that no one or few of them could undertake separately. Second, by limiting liability to the amount of capital invested by a person, the corporation became a means of furthering projects with a high risk that no one person or small group would undertake. Commercial ventures to points far from Europe and adoption of industrial techniques were such high risk projects. Had they not been accomplished by corporations, or joint stock companies, those organizations which existed before them, they might never have been carried out.

The growth of the corporation in the West is important evidence for the point that the role of economic man appeared in a structure of social relations outside the purely economic process. Economist Adolf Berle notes that the corporation was first used by "Angevin, Tudor, and Stuart kings in England, partly as a means of getting things done, partly as an extended arm of royal power."[4] Thus, political man paved the way for economic man.

Through its history, several key roles have been associated with the corporation. In the early stages of capitalism, or whenever a new area of economic activity is opened up, the dominant economic role is that of *entrepreneur*. The entrepreneur is the person who organizes the new ventures. He often risks his own capital to produce and market a new product, but he also has the skills necessary to encourage others to follow the project. Typically, the entrepreneur is most concerned with building a business and making it profitable. Once he succeeds in establishing a going concern he may lose interest in keeping it on an even keel and look for other new projects to promote. The entrepreneur is essentially a promoter. He is the kind of person, like John D. Rockefeller, Sr., who could organize the petroleum industry in the nineteenth century, or like James Ling, who organizes many-sided industrial conglomerates in the present day. While in a capitalist economy businesses are organized to make a maximum profit, it is interesting to note that the entrepreneur is often not motivated by profit. He is interested in making an organization grow and thrive in a competitive surrounding. He takes profit as an indicator of success in reaching his primary goal. Following this point, there are entrepreneurial types in many areas other than business. In academic life, an entrepreneur may found a new kind of college or a new program. The people who organized the first labor unions were entrepreneurial types willing to risk money and welfare for the success of the organization and the realization of its goal.

THE ENTREPRENEUR AND THE ORGANIZATION MAN

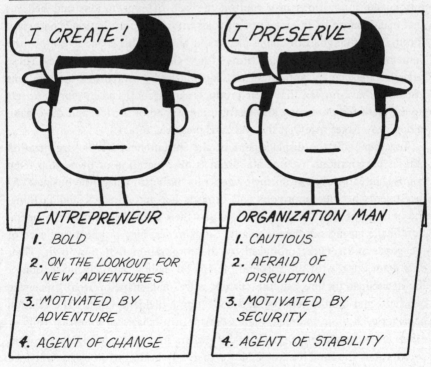

Once the enterprise is organized and has become a going concern, the major role is no longer that of entrepreneur, but that of manager or *organization man*. The skills of the entrepreneur in leading people to take risks and directing the struggle against vigorous competitors and a doubting public are no longer needed. It can even be said that giving an entrepreneur control over a going concern would be disastrous because an organized business depends on keeping up a complex network of unchanging expectations regarding markets, product types, suppliers and relations with employees. The empire-building motivations of the entrepreneur clash with the need to maintain such stable expectations. Thus, the role of organization man is the very opposite of the role of entrepreneur.

While the entrepreneur attempts to maximize, make the most, profits and growth at the cost of high risk, the organization man attempts to guarantee a stable rate of profit and to insure a predictable measure of growth by minimizing risk. The organization man is typically suspicious of undertaking new projects without impressive evidence that they will succeed. He is aware that introducing innovations may rupture the web of expectations and believes that maintenance of the structure of roles within the corporation is necessary for attaining the goals of stable profit and growth. This is one reason for the contemporary growth of small firms in new fields, such as electronics. These firms, established by entrepreneurs, are bought by established corporations after they have proven that their products can be sold. The entrepreneur sets up a system for producing and distributing a good or service, and the organization man makes sure that the system is preserved intact.

Together with the displacement of the entrepreneur by the organization man as corporations become stabilized is the separation of ownership from control. In early capitalism, the owners of a business manage the business. As investments become enormous and projects become complex and farflung, the number of stockholders increases and their direct relation to the operation of the business decreases greatly. Stockholders may not be aware even of the goods and services produced by the corporation that they own. Their only connection with the corporation may be reading the financial section of the newspaper to find out the current price of a share of stock, receiving quarterly and annual reports, and collecting a dividend check. The relation becomes even more indirect when a person owns shares in a mutual fund or other investment company. Here the owners may not even know in what corporations the fund has invested. Further, a great deal of stock in American corporations is held by other corporations, insurance companies, banks, and pension funds. Individuals have very little role to play in this kind of collective ownership.

When individual owners no longer have effective control over the operations of a corporation, professional managers responsible to a board of directors which is supposed to represent the interests of stockholders become dominant. Adolf Berle notes that these managers are not primarily concerned with seeking profit, but are motivated by improving their careers. They are organization men: "Corporation executives as individuals are not capitalists seeking profit. They are men seeking careers, in a structure offering rewards of power and position rather than profit or great wealth."[5] This does not mean that profitability is unimportant to the manager. Profitability of the firm is one yardstick by which his success in the organization is measured. Growth of the firm and the stability of its relations with other organizations are other such yardsticks.

THE SEPARATION OF OWNERSHIP FROM CONTROL

In an important study, William H. Whyte holds that the role of organization man has replaced the role of economic man as the central theme in the entire culture of the United States. In his variation of the difference between entrepreneur and manager, Whyte contrasts the *Protestant ethic* and the social ethic. The Protestant ethic, which had its roots in the doctrine that man is saved by God's grace alone, stressed hard work and worldly success as a sign of salvation. While one could not know whether or not he was saved, prosperity in the world was at least one sign that he might be favored by God. This did not mean that a person should show his success by living in luxury. Luxury was associated with sin. Seeking prosperity and avoiding luxury, many Protestants invested their money in ambitious ventures, speeding the growth of capitalism. In America, the doctrine of hard work and prosperity became separated from the idea that man is saved by God's grace alone. The central idea was that "pursuit of individual salvation through hard work, thrift, and competitive struggle is the heart of the American achievement."[6]

For Whyte, in the twentieth century it has become clear that the values of hard work, thrift, and competition do not apply in enormous organizations with job security, pension plans, and stable promotion procedures. In such organizations the social ethic appears. The *social ethic* is the idea that the individual exists as a part of society and that he finds meaning and personal worth only by cooperating with a group. In the social ethic there is the assumption that no basic conflicts occur between the individual and the organization. The social ethic interprets conflicts as misunderstandings or breakdowns in communication, which can be resolved by applying science to human relations. The role of organization man is defined by the social ethic. His major job is to keep up the network of stable expectations that was created when the organization became a going concern, and to guarantee a moderate rate of profit and growth. With these standards in mind, and with the motivation to succeed in making a career in the organization, he maintains "a belief in the group as the source of creativity; a belief in 'belongingness' as the ultimate need of the individual; and a belief in the application of science to achieve the belongingness."[7] These beliefs aid him in maintaining the network of expectations in the organization. He views these expectations as part of the group and not part of the individual. He holds that the individual should strive to make his behavior agree with the network of expectations for the benefit of the group.

Whyte holds that the social ethic is a denial of the individual. In our terms, it places too great an emphasis on the social "me," and denies the creative "I." The organization man is expected to put the feelings of the group ahead of his own plans and contributions. Holding to the social ethic does not mean taking the role of the other. In taking the role of the other a person anticipates what others in various positions will do in different situations. There is never any worship of the group, and the "I" need not act in agreement with the expectations of others. The social ethic, or role of organization man, has emerged in the setting of mammoth business corporations in which ownership is separated from control. While it is difficult to think of this role disappearing as a pattern of action in contemporary social organization, it may be possible to change it in such a way that worship of the group is decreased and responsibly taking the role of the other is increased.

LABOR ORGANIZATIONS

The same kind of historical development that has taken place in business firms has occurred in the organization of labor. In early capitalism, the worker was an individual who sold his labor to an employer. The labor contract was viewed as a bargain between two individuals, and it was voluntary and binding. If the worker was not satisfied with his conditions of employment, he could leave and get a job elsewhere. If the employer was not satisfied with the worker's performance, he could fire him and hire other workers. The major aim was to keep the labor market free so that workers could move to the jobs with highest pay and best working conditions, and employers could bid for the workers they needed.

For many reasons the free market in labor was never fully realized in practice. While nobody could force a worker to remain at an undesirable job, he might be too poor to move, too ignorant of other opportunities, or too tied emotionally and by goods to his birthplace and family. Further, the employer had a distinct advantage in the labor market because he owned and controlled the tools of production, while, in many cases, the worker had only his body and mind to offer at market. Finally, with little education, few skills, and long hours of menial labor, the worker had very little opportunity to improve himself so that he would be a more desirable product on the labor market. In view of these factors from the very beginning of capitalism there were associations of workers. An *association* is a group of people with a limited and particular purpose. Examples are labor unions, veterans organizations and clubs. They are contrasted with communities, which have many kinds of purposes.

The first labor associations were "friendly societies," in which workers pooled their resources to make sure that they received decent burials when they died and that their families would not be plunged into complete misery in case of early death. Such friendly societies flourished among skilled workers, who often owned their own tools, but were less active among factory workers and menial laborers. Friendly societies did little to improve the positions of workers in their relations with employers, but did allow many workers to avoid the worst tragedies in human existence under capitalist economies.

As opposed to the friendly society, the *labor union* is an organization with the primary purpose of gaining for its members the most favorable possible relation with employers and managers. Early labor unions met great resistance from employers in their attempts to organize workers and to win rights to bargain for wages and working conditions on behalf of their entire membership. While businesses hired private detectives to break up unions and set up "company unions" run by the employers, the most important tactic against unions was legal and political. The maintenance of a free labor market became part of the law, and the police power of the state became available to weaken labor unions. Labor unions were declared "combinations in restraint of trade" which took from the individual worker the freedom to bargain for a wage and coerced the employer. Attempts to limit the number of hours that a person had to work each day were declared illegal because they discriminated against the worker who wanted to labor more than twelve hours a day. Police were used to break up strikes and arrest labor union leaders.

INDUSTRIAL RELATIONS

With the growth of large business corporations in which ownership is separated from control and of vast government agencies, labor unions have become recognized as fundamental parts of the Western economic order. After long struggles they were granted legal standing in the United States and elsewhere in the West. In the United States and Great Britain, labor unions have been primarily *pragmatic*. In exchange for dues and loyalty they have offered their members protection of their jobs against potential competitors, protection against unfair treatment by the employer, strength in bargaining for wages and working conditions, and a means for influencing governmental policies. In Western Europe, labor unions have been weaker and more political. *Political unions* have the aim of starting basic social changes. They attempt to mobilize their memberships to replace private ownership of tools with public ownership. Since World War II, European unions have become more moderate than they were previously.

TWO KINDS OF UNION

The growth of large labor unions and their achievement of legal status and bargaining rights has changed the worker from an independent unit facing a powerful employer into an organization man. This change has brought certain benefits to business firms, in spite of the periodic disagreements between labor and management. The large labor union fits in well with the purposes of the contemporary manager to maintain a set of stable expectations. He negotiates a single contract with an organization, and can count on that organization to meet its terms. The union organizes the labor force and does not permit deviations from the contract. The manager can generally count on the fact that there will be no wildcat strikes, or unauthorized work stoppages, through the life of the contract. The union itself is run by managers who want to further their careers and to maintain a stable network of relations. While the entrepreneur views the labor union as a barrier to his goal of an empire, the organization man may see the labor union as an aid in achieving balanced growth and stable profit. When Walter Reuther, long-time president of the United Auto Workers Union, died in 1970, the presidents of the large automakers publicly announced their sorrow. This would not have happened in the age of entrepreneurs.

In the United States unions have traditionally organized blue collar workers, or workers who use tools to produce goods. White collar workers, or workers who use tools and symbols to provide services, had remained unorganized until the 1960's. This was mostly because white collar workers were considered middle class and were more likely to accept the Protestant ethic of individual achievement than blue collar workers. After World War II, trends developed that altered these considerations. First, the wages obtained by blue collar workers in strong labor unions shot ahead of the wages of many white collar workers. Second, the technological revolution in the office, increased by computers and other office machines, made much white collar work resemble blue collar work. These two trends reached maturity in the 1960's and today the new frontier of labor union organizing is among white collar workers such as insurance salesmen, clerks, teachers, social workers, government employees, and even stockbrokers.

Neither labor unions nor business firms are normally democratic in the sense that members or stockholders have some control over their operation through voting in elections between two or more choices of programs or sets of leaders, each of which has a reasonable chance of influencing decisions. Most business firms and labor unions are one-party systems run by professional managers. Sometimes two groups will compete for control of a corporation by suggesting opposing slates of directors. The small stockholders have almost no say in which slate wins, although large stockholders can exert important influence. Sometimes opposing slates of candidates will contest union elections. In at least one union, the International Typographical Union, there is a thriving two-party system. However, in the large industrial unions the one-party system is the rule. Lack of democracy in corporations and unions has been excused by two arguments: first, that these are special purpose organizations in which wide agreement on goals and policies exists; and second, that unity of leadership is necessary to permit the union or business firm to succeed in its competition with other organizations. These arguments may not be persuasive when one considers that governments can seem to be united to the rest of the world in spite of internal divisions, and that agreement on policy in enormous organizations is probably a myth.

EFFECTS OF ECONOMIC ORGANIZATIONS

The large organizations that dominate contemporary economies in the West have affected human existence in three deep-seated ways. First, they have provided the setting for the development and use of ever more sophisticated, complex, and far-reaching technologies. Second, they have provided a wide range of goods to those who can afford them and have, therefore, started a consumer revolution and a vigorous demand for goods by those living in relative poverty. Third, as a consequence of using advanced technologies on a large scale and of producing a vast number of different consumer goods, business firms and their work forces have created a crisis in the physical and organic environment of human beings. Each of the three consequences of large economic organization is interrelated with the others.

Some people claim that Americans live in a technological society. It is more accurate to say that they live in a society of large organizations using advanced technologies. The telephone system is a marvel of technological achievement, but it could not be coordinated and the technologies could not even be financed and developed without organization. This does not mean that organization determines technology, but that technology could not develop without the development of organizations at the same time. By putting their resources behind sophisticated technologies, business firms have been able to produce more goods and a wider variety of goods than has been possible ever before in history. They have also furthered the specialization of work and the division of tasks into small parts patterned by equipment.

The vast quantity of goods produced by business firms deploying advanced technologies has led economists like John Kenneth Galbraith to call the United States an affluent society. Galbraith claims that the economy, organized into business firms, labor unions, and government agencies which limit one another's power, is geared to provide the individual consumer with a maximum number of goods. This argument has met with two strong objections. First, social critic Michael Harrington has argued that there is an "other America" populated by nonwhite minority groups, the aged, and many white rural Americans who live in poverty rather than affluence. The consumer society only works for those who have positions in and are protected by the large organizations. It passes by all of the others. Second, lawyer and consumer advocate Ralph Nader has argued that the goods provided to affluent Americans are often very poor in quality, dangerous, and sold by false and misleading advertising. These debates have cast doubt on the operation of the American economy by gigantic business firms, labor unions, and government agencies.

Finally, the industrial activity necessary to provide goods to those who can afford them has created drastic pollution of the air, water, and land. Corporations, designed to achieve stable growth and profit, have not viewed contributions to clean air and water, and usable land, as a responsibility. Government agencies, accustomed to performing traditional services, have also not taken responsibility. Individual consumers have also not shown responsible behavior, but their contribution to the crisis is less serious than that of organizations. Massive environmental pollution is a consequence of massive economic organizations working on the principle of maintaining stable expectations. Thus, the problem of lessening pollution is a problem of redefining economic roles so that responsibility for the environmental consequences of economic activities is included in these roles.

SUMMARY

Modern economies in the West have shown a historical progression from individual ability to make a first step to management within large-scale organizations. Along with this change has come a shift in the central economic roles from rational economic man to organization man, and, more specifically, from entrepreneur to manager. The allocation of scarce resources in countries like the United States is not carried out mainly through countless individual decisions to buy and to sell, to produce and to consume, to employ and to work. Resources are apportioned by organizations seeking predictable growth and profit, in the case of business firms, and membership in the case of labor unions. Large business firms can control their markets through advertising, pricing policies, and new technological creations. While the American economy has produced a never previously equalled amount of consumer goods, it has left many people in poverty, has produced many inferior goods, and has led to pollution of the environment. Solutions to these problems demand new role definitions.

The quest for new role definitions leads one to think about the political process, or the ways in which human activities are controlled. The problems created by economic organizations are in great part political, because they have to do with the claims of competing human activities and how these claims can be brought together.

Notes

[1] Herbert A. Simon, *Administrative Behavior*, (New York: The Macmillan Company, 1960), p. xxv.

[2] Simon, *Administrative Behavior*, p. xxv.

[3] Simon, *Administrative Behavior* p. xxv.

[4] Edward S. Mason, (ed.), *The Corporation in Modern Society* (Cambridge: Harvard University Press, 1959), p. x.

[5] Adolf A. Berle, Jr., *Power Without Property* (New York: Harcourt Brace Jovanovich, Inc., 1959), p. 68.

[6] William H. Whyte, Jr., *The Organization Man* (Garden City: Doubleday & Company, Inc., 1957), p. 5.

[7] Whyte, *The Organization Man*, p. 7.

Suggested Readings

Aron, R. *Industrial Society*, New York: Simon & Schuster, Inc., 1968 (paper).

Berle, A. A. *Power Without Property: A New Development in American Political Economy*, New York: Harcourt Brace Jovanovich, Inc., 1959 (paper).

Drucker, P. F. *The Age of Discontinuity*, New York: Harper & Row, Publishers, 1968.

Friedman, M. *Capitalism and Freedom*, Chicago: The University of Chicago Press, 1962 (paper).

Galbraith, J. K. *The New Industrial State*, New York: New American Library of World Literature, Inc., 1968 (paper).

Harrington, M. *The Other America: Poverty in the United States*, New York: Penguin Books, Inc., 1962 (paper).

Heilbroner, R. *Worldly Philosophers*, revised edition, New York: Simon & Schuster, Inc., 1967 (paper).

Lipset, S. M. *et al.*, *Union Democracy*, Garden City: Doubleday & Company, Inc., 1956 (paper).

Rostow, W. W. *The Stages of Economic Growth: A Non-Communist Manifesto*, New York: Cambridge University Press, 1960 (paper).

Whyte, W. H. *The Organization Man*, Garden City: Doubleday & Company, Inc., 1957 (paper).

CHAPTER SIX: POLITICAL ROLES

The study of *politics* treats those social processes involved with the adjustment of relations among the different human activities. In the words of political scientist Arthur F. Bentley, politics is representative activity (activity which represents something else) because it concerns the claims of other human activities for rights and duties. For example, a political question arises when some students claim the right to shut down the university during a demonstration, while other students claim the right to attend class. Behind this is a debate as to whether the role of student should include social activism or only pursuit of studies. Thus, politics is the central arena in which the meetings between competing role definitions occur. From another point of view, but saying the same thing, politics can be considered as the care of entire communities of human beings. Here one is looking at the ways in which competing claims for rights are settled and adjusted, rather than the ways in which they are expressed and acted upon. For example, the administration may decide that the students who want to go to class will have their way. The French political scientist Maurice Duverger has defined clearly the two major viewpoints on politics: "According to one, politics is conflict, a struggle in which power allows those who possess it to ensure their hold on society and to profit by it. According to the other view, politics is an effort to bring about the rule of order and justice, in which power guarantees the general interest and the common good against the pressures of private interests."[1]

The differences between the definitions of politics as a struggle for power and politics as a process of maintaining human communities are not as great as they may first appear. Both viewpoints include the idea that political activity treats the claims of other human activities for rights. When one looks at politics as a struggle for power, he looks at the process from the viewpoint of those who are demanding rights. For example, he would look at the competing claims of the students. When one looks at politics as the maintenance of communities, he looks at the process from the viewpoint of those who are deciding among competing demands for rights. For example, he would look at the administration's decision about the student claims. This does not mean that the decisions among competing demands are always just and in the common good. Like the other social sciences, political science is divided into empirical and normative branches. *Empirical political scientists* study how demands are presented and conflicts are settled among human beings. *Normative political scientists* attempt to determine the principles by which one can discover whether or not decisions are just and in the common good. Particular decisions settling competing claims for rights may or may not be just, depending upon the principles invoked.

Political processes appear when there are competing definitions of role presented by different groups and these groups apply violence, goods, symbols, or procedures to enforce the definition that they favor. An example of political processes in action is the current debate and conflict over environmental pollution. This conflict is not primarily one about technology itself, but is chiefly concerned with the rights and duties of those who use technologies and products. It is a conflict about the rights and duties of industrial managers, public officials, and consumers. People like Ralph Nader state the argument that the role of industrial manager should be redefined to include an obligation not to pollute the environment, and that new roles for public officials should be created to enforce these obligations. Nader's opponents answer that the proper role of an industrial manager is to make profits for stockholders and that the role of the consumer should be redefined to include obligations not to misuse products and to buy only goods that do not cause pollution. Various methods are used by both sides in this conflict. People who want to place the burden of pollution control on industry have used violence, as in some sections of California where gasoline stations have been destroyed; goods, as in boycotts of firms that pollute; symbols, as in the propaganda of the ecology movement and its appeals for a "clean" environment; and procedures, as in the many legal suits brought against firms that pollute. Similarly, the people who would be harmfully affected by a new and broader definition of industrial responsibility have used a wide variety of means in the conflict. They have called in police to break up groups of trespassers, continued to produce such goods as nonreturnable bottles, distributed propaganda about how much they have done to remedy pollution, and fought through the courts to maintain their traditional rights. In this conflict, like in other political conflicts, role definitions are at stake, and the procedures of conflict and means of enforcement vary over the entire range of social control techniques. Thus, politics is representative activity because it concerns the claims of human activities for rights and duties.

POLITICAL MAN

In the past, political scientists have worked with a role of the human being known as political man. Like the notion of economic man, the idea of political man is a model to which no actual human being has ever conformed. The model has been used to show what kind of world it would be if everyone was out to gain power. While not as culturally important as economic man, political man has had an important influence on Western thought up to the present.

Economic man was said to attempt to maximize the satisfaction of his preferences. *Political man* is said to try to establish control over his living conditions so that he can satisfy some of his preferences. The political philosopher most closely associated with the idea of political man is Thomas Hobbes. Hobbes, who wrote in the seventeenth century, presented a description of the human condition in which men lived in continual fear of one another as long as they did not have a superior power above them to make rules and to see that they were enforced, by violence if necessary. Hobbes called the situation in which people lived without a superior power the *state of nature*, and claimed that the state of nature is a war of all men against all others.

Hobbes held that the war of all against all stemmed from the fact that people can never be sure of one another's intentions. If a person has control over some tools or goods, he cannot be sure that someone else will not try to take them away or even take his life. Faced with the situation of constant danger of attack from others, Hobbes argues that each person in the state of nature will attempt to gain as much control over other people as possible. He will enter a ceaseless quest for power after power. For Hobbes, more fundamental than the drive to maximize the satisfaction of one's preferences is the drive to insure that some preferences will be satisfied at all. With everyone engaged in preventive war with everyone else, the only way of gaining peace and the opportunity to satisfy preferences is for a superior power to arise that will use violence as an ultimate means to enforce stable role expectations. There will be peace when this superior power is present, not because people have lost their fear of one another, but because they fear the superior power even more.

The role of political man as one who seeks as much control over others as he can gain so that he will be able to satisfy some of his preferences, enters Western thought through Hobbes. Hobbes and many other political scientists have argued that the role of political man is more fundamental than the role of economic man. Until there is peace and some guarantee that expectations will be met, such as the expectation that one will not be murdered, there is little room for the rational figuring of costs and benefits. This view is correct in the sense that people individually figuring their advantages would be unlikely to keep up a set of stable expectations. But this means that there must be orderly ways of deciding among competing claims for rights, not that the role of political man is more important than the role of economic man. The role of political man is just as distorted and oversimplified as the role of economic man.

People only approach the model of political man in their own lives at certain critical times in social life. Mainly, the role of political man becomes widely taken and performed in periods where role exploitation is widespread. *Role exploitation* is the practice of attempting to maximize the rights associated with the role that one is performing at a certain time and to minimize the obligations associated with it. It is the attempt to take advantage of one's position. For example, the auto mechanic who uses his position to charge for repairs that are not needed is engaged in role exploitation. When everyone attempts to take advantage of his position at once, something like a war of all against all occurs, and people begin to take and perform the role of political man. For example, the auto mechanic may charge for unnecessary repairs, but the driver may claim that the mechanic performed shoddy work and caused an accident that was really caused by poor driving. Role exploitation only takes place within a context of role definitions that are enforced by means other than mere violence. These role definitions are built into the "me" during the process of socialization. The war of all against all and the emergence of political man does not take place when there is conflict between cultures over role definitions. In cultural conflicts, the groups involved are united within themselves on the role definitions preferred. Cultural conflicts are group conflicts. Political man appears only when a single culture is collapsing because of widespread role exploitation. When cultures collapse people see no reason to fulfill their obligations. When there is role exploitation there is no trust, when there is no trust there is no social bond, and when there is no social bond there is war of all against all. The relation of political man to the study of political processes is the same as the relation of economic man to economic processes. Just as the roles through which resources are assigned are far more complex than the role of economic man, the roles through which conflicts over role definitions are carried on and settled are far more complex than the role of political man.

FORMS OF GOVERNMENT

Roles through which conflicts over role definitions are carried on and settled are related to one another in forms of government. *Forms of government* can be defined as the ways in which disputes over various demands for rights are settled. All organizations are, in part, governments because they have roles for expressing and resolving conflicts. However, not all organizations are states. *States* are organizations which control the uses of violence permitted by formal rules over a specific territory and population. There are people who have government who are not members of a state, particularly many preliterate groups. The study of political science includes far more than the investigation of states. It encompasses the study of preliterate stateless societies, the political and governmental aspects of organizations, and the relations among states.

The form of government typical of the modern West is democracy. At its most basic, *democracy* is a method of deciding between competing role definitions by a majority vote of those involved in the conflict. At this fundamental level, democracy can be distinguished from three other methods of making decisions. First, there is decision by *lot*, in which a choice is randomly selected from among those choices presented. Decision by lot is often used in choosing people to perform tasks about which there is little conflict. It was used extensively by the ancient Greeks.

THREE WAYS OF MAKING DECISIONS

Second, there is *autocratic* decision—decision by some specific person or group, which has been specified in advance. This method of decision has been the most extensively used in world history. Autocratic systems have been based on a wide variety of principles, ranging from divine right to superior knowledge. Most widespread have been systems in which the role of decision maker is given to a person because of his birth. However, in the contemporary world autocratic systems usually place the power of decision in the hands of groups of people who are believed to be specially qualified to govern. Communist governments, which claim that they rule in the interests of the workers, and military dictatorships, which claim that they rule in the lasting interests of the nation, are examples of contemporary autocracies.

Third, there is *anarchy*—the system in which no social method of decision making exists. Under anarchy, each person is his own rolemaker, and conflicts among competing role definitions are resolved through voluntary agreement, control of goods, or superior force. There are no procedures.

MODERN DEMOCRACY

No actual democratic government works merely on the principle of majority rule. The democratic governments that have appeared in the West since the eighteenth century have departed formally from strict majority rule in three different ways. In any group larger than one whose members can meet on a face to face basis, direct rule by the majority on each issue that confronts the group is difficult. Consequently the device of representation has been applied in modern democratic governments. Modern democracies are *representative democracies*. Since the principle of rule by the majority does not include guarantees that the majority will preserve its own rule and protect the rights of minorities to become majorities, the device of constitutionalism has been applied in modern democratic governments. Modern democracies are *constitutional democracies*. Since the majority may not always obey the constitutional limits, some democratic governments include a Supreme Court which is supposed to guard the constitutional rules. Some modern democracies contain *judicial review* of laws passed by the representatives of the majority. Thus, actual democracies formally limit majority rule through representation, constitutions, and sometimes judicial review.

Representation in a democracy means that the majority chooses people to make laws for the community. *Laws* are rules specifying rights and duties which are made according to procedures contained in the constitution. For example, a law requiring employers to contribute to insurance plans for workers is a partial definition of the role of employer. Laws are settlements of disputes over role definitions. The law requiring insurance contributions may have followed a struggle between labor and management. A constitution is a set of rules stating how laws should be made, and a set of limitations on the subjects that can be covered by laws. For example, according to the United States Constitution no law can be made abridging (limiting) the free practice of religion. Thus, in a representative and constitutional democracy, people elected by majorities make rules (laws) for a community in agreement with procedures (constitutional principles) stating how these rules should be made and principles stating what subjects these rules should cover. Another way of putting this is that constitutions define the roles of the representatives and other officials, while laws define roles outside of the central political process.

Each of the three limitations on the majority principle has caused difficulties in democratic thought. While direct majority rule would be impossible in large organizations, there are problems with representation. Can the majority give away its authority over decisions to a representative without defeating itself? Even if there is periodic reelection there is no guarantee that the representative will not act against the wishes of the majority, even if he could decide them. A President elected because he promised to end a war may expand that war. Once the representative is removed from those who have elected him it is difficult for the majority to know whether or not he is faithful to its interests. There is even some dispute about whether the representative should attempt to follow the dictates of those who have elected him or decide according to wider interests or decide according to his conscience. Representation does seem to place a limit on abuses of decision-making power, but it does not guarantee that the wishes of majorities will be expressed in laws.

Constitutionalism presents another set of problems. To set limits on the laws preferred by the majority is to distrust majority rule in some respects. Bills of rights prohibiting laws limiting freedom of speech, worship, assembly, and other acts considered necessary to allow minorities to become majorities peacefully may be both wise and moral social inventions, but they do limit majority rule. Democracy contains this important contradiction: if democracy is to function successfully and allow peaceful change, it must include safeguards against certain possible consequences of majority rule. At the very least, democracies must protect themselves against majorities that would abolish majority rule. At their fullest, democracies must make provisions to insure that minorities can remain members of the community and act peacefully to gain majority support. Nothing in the principle of majority rule stops a majority from declaring that all the members of a racial minority be killed by the state. Yet modern democracies provide safeguards against such actions. None of these safeguards can be justified by the principle of majority rule itself, but depend on judgments about the nature of the good life. One such judgment is that people should not be killed because of their skin color.

Judicial review presents the greatest problems to the majority principle. Judicial review means that a person or small group (Supreme Court) is given the role of determining whether or not the laws passed by the representatives of the voters are in agreement with the constitution. In judicial review, the chosen person or group decides whether or not particular laws cover subjects prohibited by the constitution and whether or not they have been made in agreement with the procedures defined in the constitution. For example, judges may decide whether or not a certain law really does limit the free practice of religion. Judicial review is another important limitation on majority rule which cannot be defended by the principle of majority rule. It can only be justified by judgments on the nature of the good life. Thus, modern democracies in the West are historical institutions, partly including the principle of majority rule and partly including other principles such as guaranteed civil rights and representation.

MODERN DEMOCRACIES ARE REPRESENTATIVE AND CONSTITUTIONAL

BUREAUCRACY

Parallel to the method of democracy in making rules is the method of *bureaucracy* in applying them to conditions in the human world. Once a law has been passed defining rights and duties, some way must be set up to put these rights and duties into effect and to enforce them. For example, if there is a law passed requiring business firms to avoid polluting water with mercury and setting up roles to enforce that law, these roles must be filled by people and must be carried out if the law is to become a factor in human behavior. There are two general ways in which the roles defined in laws can be filled and carried out. The person filling the role can be given the role as his personal property, or he can be given a salary for performing his duties. These choices can be illustrated by the example of enforcing antipollution laws. The person given the role of enforcement could have the duty of investigating violations of the law and the right to keep as personal income the fines that he could collect. In this case the role would be his personal property. As a choice, or alternative, the person given the role of enforcement could be paid a salary for investigating violations of the law and for bringing violators to court. In this case, ownership of the role would be separate from performance of it. Fines would go to the state. Democracies have normally separated ownership from performance, although in the United States many justices of the peace own their roles in the sense that their incomes are derived from the payment of traffic fines and marriage fees.

TWO WAYS OF FILLING ADMINISTRATIVE ROLES

In filling the roles defined by laws another set of alternatives is very important. The person can be chosen to fill the role on the basis of a demonstration of his ability to perform it or on the basis of some characteristic which he has that is unrelated to the skills required by performance. In the case of the person enforcing antipollution laws, he could be chosen because of his legal training and high achievement on a civil service examination (ability), or because he is white and is a relative of a prominent public official (characteristics unrelated to ability). In democracies, the tendency has been to fill the roles defined in laws on the basis of ability to perform them. However, in the United States many public offices are staffed by people who belong to and work for the political party in office and who may or may not have special abilities for performing their duties.

Other factors relating to the performance of roles defined in laws are concerned with the general nature of the rights and duties contained in the roles. There is an important choice between the alternatives of defining the rights and duties of the role very broadly and defining them narrowly and specifically. For example, the person filling the role of enforcing antipollution laws could be given very broadly defined powers of investigation and arrest, and could be given many other duties besides enforcing antipollution laws. As an alternative, his role could be sharply defined, including only enforcement of one particular law and limited powers of investigation and arrest. Democracies have tended to define roles specifically, creating a complex division of labor and limited powers. However, this is not always the case. The role of a cabinet member in the United States is not sharply defined, and neither is the role of the director of a powerful agency such as the Federal Bureau of Investigation.

Another important choice in role definition is whether the person should apply general rules in his work regardless of who is involved, or whether he should make exceptions to the rules in certain cases. Here the person enforcing antipollution laws could either treat all violators in the same way or make exceptions in certain cases, such as when the violator is a contributor to a powerful political party. Democracies have tended to support formally the principle that exceptions to the rules based on favoritism should not be made. In practice this principle has been applied unevenly. For example, well-to-do people who become publicly intoxicated are driven home frequently by police and politely told to get some sleep while poor people in the same condition are put in jail for the night. The meaning of law is destroyed if there is too much favoritism in its enforcement, but in all large-scale systems there is a degree of such favoritism. Role exploitation becomes widespread when favoritism gets out of control.

Bureaucracy is a method of administration, or a way of putting the rights and duties defined in laws into practice. It is the administrative system in which the ownership of an office is separated from the discharge of its duties, and people are chosen to fill roles by their ability to perform them. Also, rights and duties are defined specifically, and favoritism does not distort the application of rules. Bureaucracies are also hierarchies in which roles are arranged on a ladder of authority. One obeys the person ahead of him in the chain of command because he is legally entitled to command. Ultimately, however, one obeys because he accepts the way in which decisions are made, or the form of government.

Bureaucracies are the most efficient organizations devised by human beings for carrying out large-scale projects. By separating the performance of role from ownership of the office, they insure that movements to defeat the purposes of the entire organization will be kept at a minimum. By selecting people to fill roles on the basis of ability, they contribute directly to gaining organizational goals. By defining roles specifically, they create a division of labor that allows complex and far-reaching tasks to be performed. Without this division of labor, tasks could not be performed that are beyond the understanding of any single individual. By creating a system in which favoritism in the carrying out of rules is held to a minimum, they further the stability of role expectations.

BUREAUCRAT

All kinds of organizations can be bureaucratic. Contemporary business firms in which ownership is separated from control and managers supervise complex operations are bureaucratic. The parts of labor unions devoted to bargaining, managing pension funds, organizing new workers, maintaining union property, and providing recreational, medical, and cultural services to members are bureaucratic. Government agencies charged with putting laws into effect are bureaucratic and so are military services, universities, and hospitals. In present-day America more and more people spend their working lives in bureaucracies. They perform specialized tasks for a salary and may lose sight of their roles as human beings and of their creative "I." The dangers of following bureaucratic commands blindly and losing sight of one's role as a human being are illustrated by the war criminals of the twentieth century who have excused their participation in slaughter and torture by saying, "I was only following orders." Instead of taking the role of human being they took the role of their superior in the bureaucracy. The dangers of stiffly following bureaucratic routines and losing the creative "I" are illustrated by the organization men who cannot live outside of the protection of their bureaucracies and who fear any change in their lives. In the twentieth century bureaucracies are the central arenas for the interplay between the creative "I" and the social "me."

Bureaucracies carry many dangers with them. First, there is the danger that by following the rules strictly and rigidly the bureaucrat will become insensitive to the feelings of those he affects. Hospital personnel who are overly concerned that all the proper forms get filled out and that the patient will be able to pay his bills have severely upset many people needing emergency treatment. Second, there is the danger that bureaucracies will lose sight of their original purpose and turn their attention mainly to preserving themselves and growing for the sake of growing. Churches which become involved in administering their property and forgetting the needs of their members, and universities which expand their programs and forget about the needs of their students are examples of this tendency. Related to growth for the sake of growth is the danger that bureaucracies will block necessary changes. It took a long and hard battle before the American military was ready to take aviation seriously. Finally, there is the danger that bureaucracies will not be responsible to the public. Bureaucracies tend to keep as much secret as possible. For example, the Department of Agriculture is reluctant to release lists of those who get the highest payments from the farm program. How can bureaucracies be accountable if nobody on the outside even knows what they are doing?

Bureaucracies, while associated with the development of democratic forms of government, are neither democratic themselves nor are they found only in democracies. Much of life in the Communist countries is bureaucratized and fascist regimes like Nazi Germany were dependent upon bureaucratic administration to realize their policies. Bureaucracy is a method that can be used by any modern government, whether public or private, to administer its affairs. The important determinant, or determining factor, of what happens in a bureaucracy is outside of the bureaucracy itself. Whatever group stands at the top of the bureaucracy will control it. If that group represents an autocracy like the Communist Party or a clique of military leaders, the bureaucracy will do its bidding. If the group represents a majority of voters, the bureaucracy will similarly do its bidding. Of course, no bureaucracy is a perfect tool. Those who fill bureaucratic roles will resist interference with their powers and routines even by those in command.

The main relation of bureaucracy to democracy is that bureaucracy is an efficient means for putting the policies of the majority into action. Since bureaucracy is not inherently biased for or against any policy it can shift its activities with changes in majority preference better than other forms of organization can shift theirs. Also both democracy and bureaucracy tend to emphasize equality. In a democracy everyone's vote is equal. In an ideal bureaucracy, every case is treated in agreement with general rules and no exceptions are made on the basis of favoritism. However, a bureaucracy is by no means a democracy. Bureaucracies are like dictatorships in the sense that the people who fill roles in them do not determine what the organization will do. They are assigned to certain tasks, and in return for a salary and a measure of job security, they are expected to perform those tasks and to follow the orders of their superiors when these deal with matters covered by the rules. Thus, there is a question as to whether democracy and bureaucracy are consistent with one another in the long run. The kind of person who is the ideal democratic citizen is critical and questioning about roles and is willing to take responsibility for making decisions. The ideal bureaucratic person is a specialist in a narrow area who follows his assigned role obediently. Can a person be both democrat and bureaucrat? It is too easy to say that the majority decides and the bureaucracy obeys.

Both democracy and bureaucracy are ideal types. In no actual democracy do the representatives perfectly reflect the preferences of the majority and stay completely within the bounds of constitutional limits. In all bureaucracies some people use their offices for personal profit. Some people are employed for reasons other than their abilities to perform specialized roles. Some people are given vague and far-reaching powers. And some people decide cases on the basis of personal favoritism or dictates of power.

Cutting across both democracies and bureaucracies are *interest groups*, groups formed to promote laws on one topic, which affect the operation of both structures. Political parties are organizing interest groups and blocs of voters. The political processes of the modern West have been characterized by formal representative and constitutional democracy as the way of making decisions, formal bureaucracy as the way of carrying out decisions, and interest groups and parties as the ways of influencing the content of decisions and the extent to which they are carried out.

INTEREST GROUPS AND PARTIES

The vital element in decision making in contemporary Western democracies is not the individual voter but the interest group. The *interest group* is an organization that is concerned to make specific role definitions part of the law and to see that these definitions are enforced. The organizations promoting the movement for a cleaner environment are examples of interest groups. The Earth Day movement, the wildlife federations, and the conservation groups attempt to have laws passed which will increase the duties of consumers and industrial managers to maintain a pollution-free environment. They also attempt to see that these laws are enforced. Associations in various industries fight back by attempting to block passage of such laws and to convince administrators to act on a very narrow definition of the laws.

Interest groups act to influence policy and administration in several ways. First, they attempt to influence public opinion by making public statements, holding demonstrations, and distributing propaganda. A favorable climate of public opinion may sway representatives to support laws proposed by the interest group out of fear that they will lose votes if they are not active in support. Second, interest groups attempt to get the backing of other interest groups for their proposals. Manufacturers will enlist the support of labor unions concerned with their industry in struggles to restrict foreign competition and moves to get large government contracts. Third, interest groups will continually be present at legislatures to influence representatives to support their programs. This is not done mainly by bribing representatives but by providing them with information, introductions to important people, and political advice and aid. Fourth, interest groups will continually be present in bureaucracies administering laws, cooperating with administrators in return for consideration of their policies. Fifth, interest groups will go to court, attempting to block or speed administration of laws that affect them. Sixth, interest groups will sometimes be designated by a law as the agent to carry out that law. Thus, in some states in the United States committees of the bar association, representing lawyers, have authority in the process of selecting judges.

Interest groups play a decisive role in our present-day democracies. Interests that are not organized and do not act in the six ways detailed above are not likely to gain satisfaction in the political arena. This is the reason struggles to organize nonwhite minority groups, poor people, women, students, welfare recipients, and the aged have been so important in contemporary politics. While voting is still a central process in selecting representatives, well organized and financed interest groups can affect voting patterns through campaigns to influence public opinion. If such groups lose at the polls, they can still try to influence representatives, administrators, judges, and other interest groups to accept their points of view. Since contemporary political processes are a far more complex affair than majorities making a decision and bureaucracies carrying it out, interest groups have a wide range in which to operate. Once an interest group is legally entitled to administer a law, it is nearly impossible to dislodge it.

Interest groups cannot simply be treated as organizations out to take advantage of the public. They are responses to the massive scale of social activity made possible by sophisticated technologies, specialized symbol systems, complex rules, and a wide variety of products. They try to gain the rights of specialized parts of human activity against the claims of other specialities. They organize public opinion and preference around such specialities and they must be harmonized by other organizations.

In Western democracies the *political party* performs the role of harmonizing the claims of interest groups. The party is an organization that attempts to arrange a majority of votes for its candidates so that these candidates will become public officials. In competing for majority preference the parties must satisfy the claims of strong interest groups and balance them against one another. Thus, the most important role is that of the *broker*, a politician who attempts to put together enough interest groups to insure a majority of votes. Through the activity of brokers the claims of the best organized interest groups are given a hearing. This does not mean that the preferences of majorities on issues are satisfied. The number of issues on which decisions are made is so large that no election can be considered an indication of majority preference on most issues. Further, many people do not vote and even more know little or nothing about the major issues. In this situation, interest groups become important influences on parties and other aspects of the political process.

Political life in contemporary Western democracies is very impersonal. The major actors in the political process are interest groups, political parties, and government agencies, all of which are bureaucratized to at least some extent. Majorities are not formed from a multitude of individual decisions based on calculation of personal or public interest. They are formed from habit, party affiliation, membership in interest groups, exposure to propaganda, and the personal appeal of candidates. When majorities are shown during elections, it is frequently not clear what particular policies they favor. The fragile connection between voting and the process of making and applying laws has led to a crisis in contemporary democracies. During the 1960's new groups, such as youth, racial minorities, and women, began to organize interest groups in

THE SEPARATION OF VOTING FROM CONTROL

earnest to favor changes in the role definitions of those who control the massive bureaucracies. They have used a wide variety of tactics ranging from violence to persuasion, and their opponents have answered in kind. At this point it is difficult to predict what effects the new political movements will have on the practice of democracy, but they have already begun to alter the relation between democracy and bureaucracy in the direction of decentralization, or away from centralized government.

SUMMARY

Politics is the social process that concerns the claims of human activities for rights and duties. Thus, politics is the arena for competition between different role definitions and for the settlement of this competition. The element of struggle in the political process has led some political scientists to make the role of political man central in their study. Political man, who lives in continual fear that others will not permit his plans, constantly seeks power so that he will be able to have the peace to satisfy some of his preferences.

Political man does not appear in society normally, but does enter human existence when large numbers of people exploit their roles by attempting to maximize rights and minimize duties.

Actual political roles are much more complex than the role of political man. The political process is organized into forms of government and methods of administration. In the modern West, representative and constitutional democracy has been the typical form of government, and bureaucracy has been the typical method of administration. Democracies, working by the principle of majority rule combined with guaranteed rights, and bureaucracies, working by the principles of specialization and rule of law, have been profoundly influenced by interest groups and political parties. Interest groups present the demands of a particular sector of social life for rights and duties. Parties balance the claims of interest groups against one another so that they can gain a majority of votes. The impersonal nature of contemporary political processes has led, in the 1960's and 1970's, to widespread movements for decentralization and the recognition of new groups.

In pressing their claims, both new and old groups attempt to communicate with the public and to influence the educational system. The next chapter will examine the importance of communication and education.

Notes

[1] Maurice Duverger, *The Idea of Politics* (Chicago: Henry Regnery Co., 1964), p. 12.

Suggested Readings

Almond, G. A. and Verba, S. *Civic Culture: Political Attitudes and Democracy in Five Nations*, Boston: Little, Brown and Company, 1965 (paper).

Blau, P. M. *Bureaucracy in Modern Society*, New York: Random House, Inc., 1956 (paper).

Dahl, R. *Who Governs: Democracy and Power in an American City*, New Haven: Yale University Press, 1961 (paper).

Eulau, H. *The Behavioral Persuasion in Politics*, New York: Random House, Inc., 1963 (paper).

Friedrich, C. J. *Man and His Government*, New York: McGraw-Hill Book Company, 1963.

Lasswell, H. *Politics: Who Gets What, When, and How*, Cleveland: Meridian Press, 1958 (paper).

Lipset, S. M. *Political Man: The Social Bases of Politics*, Garden City: Doubleday & Company, Inc., 1963 (paper).

Mills, C. W. *The Power Elite*, New York: Oxford University Press, 1959 (paper).

Neustadt, R. *Presidential Power*, New York: New American Library of World Literature, Inc., 1964 (paper).

Zeigler, H. *Interest Groups in American Society*, New York: Prentice Hall, Inc., 1964.

CHAPTER SEVEN: EDUCATION AND COMMUNICATION

Communication is the transfer of information about cultural objects and other aspects of the world from one person to another. The content of communication is symbolic and the form of communication is a medium. For example, this book is composed of words on the medium of the printed page. In communication, symbols, such as those of language, are passed on from one person to another through such media as newsprint, radio waves, transmitters and receivers, and photographs. Communication is one of the four general and interrelated social processes without which human beings could have no culture, social relations, or personal development. The other processes are economics, centering on the use of tools and the allocation of resources; politics, concerning the relation of human activities to one another and the putting to use of rules; and appreciation, relating to the enjoyment of products and the maintenance of human solidarity. The processes of economics, politics, and appreciation could not go on in the absence of communication. People learn how to use tools through symbolic instruction, rules are expressed in symbols, and symbolic directions are necessary to the selection and full enjoyment of products. Even when a person is alone, communication is not absent. People think by talking to themselves, and speech is symbolic. Human thought is a dialogue in which one part of the self presents a proposal symbolically and another part of the self responds to this proposal. An interesting experiment is to attempt to think outside of a dialogue. One will find that there is always someone who suggests and someone who listens. Even the individual self is social in the sense that it cannot think and plan outside of a dialogue.

The self is also social and dependent upon communication in yet another way. Before a person can think and plan, suggest and respond, he must have a supply of symbols with which he can represent objects, experiences, and actions which are not in his immediate presence. A person can think of where he will drive the next day even if he is not looking at his car. A symbol is a thing whose value or meaning is given to it by those who use it. Human beings can create new symbols within the context of symbol systems, like languages or systems of musical notation. But the individual human being, unaided by learning, cannot create entire symbol systems. A person learns to think by learning symbol systems that were present before his birth. Thus, the self is social because it cannot even come into being without the help of others who teach the child systems of symbols. Once a person has mastered a language he can begin to create new symbols and to help alter old symbol systems.

Languages are continually changing in response to the new ideas of individuals and groups of people. However, one cannot change a language without having learned it. This is only another way of saying that the creative self "I" gains its full development only after the appearance of the social self "me." When a person goes off alone to think by himself he carries society with him in the words that he uses in his interior dialogue, the discussion within himself. This does not lessen the individual so much as it places him in a context, a particular area of discussion. The individual is a contributor whose plans rework and go beyond cultural materials and whose creations find their way back into culture. The "I" would have little meaning without the "me."

Education is one key type of communications process. Education is used here to mean the social process of learning. It includes the activities of schools, as well as the many learning experiences that people have on the job, in the community, and through using the mass media. Education is the process of learning how to communicate and how to use tools, enjoy products, and apply rules. Throughout human existence education is constantly going on. When a person gets a job in an office, a factory, or anywhere else, he is taught the extent of his rights and duties and how to use the tools that will permit him to exercise those rights and perform those duties. This kind of instruction is education just as what goes on in schools is education. Further, in one's everyday life education goes on with few interruptions, and the person who is learning is often unaware of it. The advertisements on radio and television, and in the magazines and newspapers, teach people how to use products and give them information about styles of consumption that they can copy. Discussions among friends and colleagues, news reports, magazine articles and documentaries, and speeches inform people about the rules and role definitions that are proposed and applied within the culture.

Careful reading of good newspapers and news magazines can give a person a continuing education in the social sciences. Most issues discussed in newspapers, magazines, and the electronic media involve conflicts over role definitions. What should be the role of the black? Should the industrialist be given more duties in cleaning up pollution? Should congressmen have more rights in shaping foreign policy? Should the role of woman be different from the role of human being? By looking at the news as education in the area of role definitions, a person can improve his knowledge of the social sciences and his understanding of the world around him.

Most education in the use of tools, the enjoyment of products, and the application of rules takes place out of school. Traditionally, schools have specialized in communicating information about how to communicate. However, even in this area, the child has already learned to speak before he enters school. Given speaking children, the schools traditionally taught reading, writing, and arithmetic. They taught children how to use the visual symbols of the ordinary language and the visual symbols representing quantity, mathematics. Thus, they taught them how to extend their communication. Today schools have begun to teach the use of tools (vocational education), the enjoyment of products (recreation), the application of rules (student government), and the learning of a wide variety of symbol systems (musical notation, foreign languages, and specialized scientific languages). Even with all of these developments most contemporary education still goes on outside of school.

One type of education is the process of *socialization* in which the person learns first to express his demands, then to take the role of particular others, then to take the role of people who fill positions, then to take the role of human being within his culture, and finally to modify and choose among the roles available to him. In the family children learn to take the roles of particular others and to ask such questions as, "What would my mother think if I did this?" In school and among friends children learn to take the roles of people who fill positions and ask such questions as, "What would a teacher think if I did this?" As his experience broadens to more than one institution, the child learns to take the role of human being and to ask, "What would people think if I did this?" Thus, the socialization process takes place in many settings and is not closely controlled from a single center. Yet while it is somewhat haphazard, it is also the most important educational process that a human being undergoes. In the socialization process one learns to apply rules without which there would be no stable expectations of human activity and no cooperation among human beings.

LEARNING

The process of learning is developmental. It proceeds through the stages of the life history of the child. The child psychologist Piaget has defined three stages in the intellectual development of children. Up to the ages of five or six, "the child's mental work consists principally in establishing relationships between experience and action; his concern is with manipulating the world through action."[1] In this stage the child attempts to gain some confidence in the world. The child is able to use symbols, but only in a limited sense. He learns how to apply symbols to represent sense qualities, and is able to make descriptive generalizations. For example, in the first stage the child is able to identify an object as colored blue or a sound as loud. These are sense qualities. He can also identify objects as combinations of sensed qualities. For example, the child is able to identify objects such as houses and dogs. However, in the first stage the child's understanding is limited in certain important ways. He does not clearly separate actions caused by purposes from physical motions. For the child in this stage all behaviors are personally caused: "The sun moves because God pushes it, and the stars, like himself, have to go to bed."[2] The child also cannot clearly separate ends from means. It takes some time for him to learn that merely expressing a desire does not guarantee that it will be satisfied. The first steps in the direction of separating ends from means are simple attempts at trial and error. The child in the first stage of intellectual development does not think out strategies to obtain goals or criticize and compare his goals. In this stage the child learns how to name objects and quanities.

From the ages of six or seven to the ages of ten to fourteen, the child is in the second stage of intellectual development. While in the first stage the child was capable of naming objects according to their sense qualities, he could not grasp what Piaget has called the idea of reversibility. Reversibility is the notion common in mathematics or physics that behind changes in quality are constant processes or operations. For example, if a quart of milk is poured into several glasses, a physicist (or any normal person) would say that the volume of milk in the glasses added up to a quart. The child in the first stage of intellectual development could not grasp the idea of volume apart from specific sensed qualities. For him, the volume of milk in four glasses is not the same volume of milk in a quart. In the second stage of intellectual development the child does grasp the idea of reversibility in specific situations. He understands that the same quantity can take different appearances, and he can solve problems based on this understanding, such as balancing scales. He does not proceed completely by trial and error, but can figure out the kind of object that would, for example, balance a scale. The child in the second stage of intellectual development is still limited in his capability of using symbols. While he is able to use symbols for figuring out the answers to problems, he cannot understand a wide range of alternative solutions. Thus, the second stage of intellectual development is a transitional stage. The child can use the idea of reversibility and the notion that underneath changes in appearances there are constant processes and operations, but he is not fully aware of that idea in its formal statement. Thus, faced with a concrete situation, he can predict accurately that he will need more objects to balance a scale, but he will not understand the abstract ideas of mass, weight, and balance. This is why Piaget calls the second stage the stage of concrete operations. The child can use symbols to think out answers to specific problems, and can apply abstract principles in action. However, he cannot state clearly the principles that he applies. He is, therefore, strictly limited in the range of possible answers that he can consider.

The third stage of intellectual development begins between the ages of ten and fourteen. Piaget calls this stage the stage of formal operations because the child is able to grasp general ideas, such as mass, weight, and balance, apart from specific or concrete situtations, and he can apply them to new concrete situations. The child can now imagine new situations which he has never experienced before in which general ideas can be applied. He begins from the concept and works down to the situation. He grasps the constant processes behind the changing appearances. Educational psychologist Jerome Bruner remarks that it is "at this point that the child is able to give formal or axiomatic expression to the concrete ideas that before guided his problem-solving but could not be described or formally understood."[3] At this stage the child is intellectually mature, and what remains for education is to teach him how to use more complex sets of abstractions and how to apply them imaginatively to new problems.

The three stages of intellectual development closely parallel the stages of socialization. The first stage, in which the child can name sense qualities and immediately present objects, appears at the same time as the stage in which the child differentiates himself from others and is capable of expressing his demands. The second stage, in which the child is able to grasp general principles in action, even though he does not consciously understand them, parallels the stage in which the child becomes capable of taking the role of the particular other. Just as the child relates intellectually to the concrete situation in this stage, he relates socially to the particular other. The third stage, in which the child is able to understand general principles in their abstract form, corresponds to the stage in which the child becomes able to take the role of people in various positions. Just as the child learns to separate the idea of volume from particular situations in which volumes of liquid are present, he learns to separate the role of teacher from particular teachers who instruct him. It is at this point that he becomes mature socially as well as mature intellectually. In the social realm, what remains for him is to learn to take a wider variety of roles, to compare other roles, and to create new roles.

Within the stages of intellectual and social development the child progresses only through relations with others. The child will not develop naturally from one stage to the next. He must be taught how to use symbols in the ways which meet the requirements of his stage of development. This teaching is accomplished by using the methods of social control to encourage learning. In the simplest case, the very symbols that are given to the child are controlled. Most children in the United States learn English rather than French because English is spoken in their families. They learn to take certain roles because those are the roles presented to them. Beyond the mere presence of certain symbols, learning takes place through rewards and punishments both a part of and separate from what is learned. Intrinsic rewards are those immediately involved with or a part of the act of learning, such as the joy of solving a problem or the gaining the means to reach a desired end. Extrinsic rewards and punishments are those not immediately attached to or separated from the act of learning. Here one learns because he is given something that he wants, is praised, is deprived of something that he wants, is blamed, or is physically punished for performing or failing to perform a certain task, such as memorizing a multiplication table.

In the United States, grades and the rewards and punishments associated with them are the major extrinsic rewards and punishments attached to learning in school. Educational reformers are divided into two main groups. One group holds that education should be designed to replace extrinsic rewards and punishments with intrinsic rewards as much as possible. The second group holds that education should be designed to replace extrinsic punishments with extrinsic rewards as much as possible. Both groups begin with the view that education is a social process. Intellectual and social development would not take place unless people put symbols and problems in front of the child and directed him toward intrinsic rewards or applied extrinsic rewards or punishments.

THE SCHOOL

At the center of the educational process in our present-day complex societies is the school. The school, as well as the business corporation, the labor union, the representative constitutional democracy and the administrative bureaucracy, developed as human existence became more specialized. Before the arrival of primary and secondary schools most people were educated within the family and local community. No special organization was devoted to systematizing intellectual and social learning. As social life became more complex, many aspects of human existence, particularly work, came to demand people who could read, write, and do numerical calculations (mathematics). Further, democratic government and modern nondemocratic states required populations that could understand issues and policies which were beyond the range of their private, individual existence. For example, governments attempt to persuade populations to support a war effort. Without an awareness of such issues as war and peace, these governments could not gain support for far-flung projects.

Until radio and television became so popular, such understanding could best be gained through reading. The family, which was probably made up of people who could neither read, write, nor do sums, could not teach children these means of communication. Thus, the primary school arose to provide what the family could not offer and what the role definitions demanded. The primary school, which took the child through the second stage of intellectual and social development, was a specialized organization performing the new function of teaching children how to communicate in ways in which their parents could not communicate. Learning how to use tools was done on the job. Learning how to enjoy products was done in families and in groups of age mates. And learning rules and roles was done throughout social existence. The primary school arose to teach new symbols.

As the specialization and contact among cultures associated with modern times became more intense, new roles were created calling for large numbers of people who had skills more advanced than merely reading, writing, and calculating. At the same time systems of rules became more complex and demanded more penetrating understanding in people following them. New symbol systems and vocabularies were developed to describe and plan solutions to the problems created by specialization and cultural contact. Finally, the range of products and experiences open to the modern human became increased drastically.

New products, such as electrical appliances and household chemicals, carried dangers with them for those who did not know how to use them correctly. Frequent contacts between people with different cultural backgrounds led to the need to provide people with an understanding of roles different from their own. Political doctrines such as fascism and communism competed with constitutional representative democracy. Thus there developed the demand that children learn the principles of democracy, citizenship, and patriotism, so that they could prevent dictatorship.

The explosion of modern life into specialized roles and patchwork cultures disturbed the continuity of socialization. Demands arose that some agency guide the adolescent into adulthood. The new availability of art, music, and literature to large numbers of people created a call for education in the appreciation and creation of these aspects of culture. All of these developments and demands led to the growth of the secondary school, or high school.

The primary school guided the child through the second stage of intellectual development, teaching him how to communicate in new ways. The secondary school was devoted to encouraging progress in the third stage of intellectual development. In the third stage of intellectual development the child is capable of understanding systems of general ideas for themselves and using these general ideas to solve new problems. Thus, the secondary school introduces the adolescent to the major areas of culture in a relatively systematic way.

For this reason secondary schools have tended to be departmental in organization, like bureaucracies, and primary schools have tended to leave all

THE GROWTH OF REASON ?

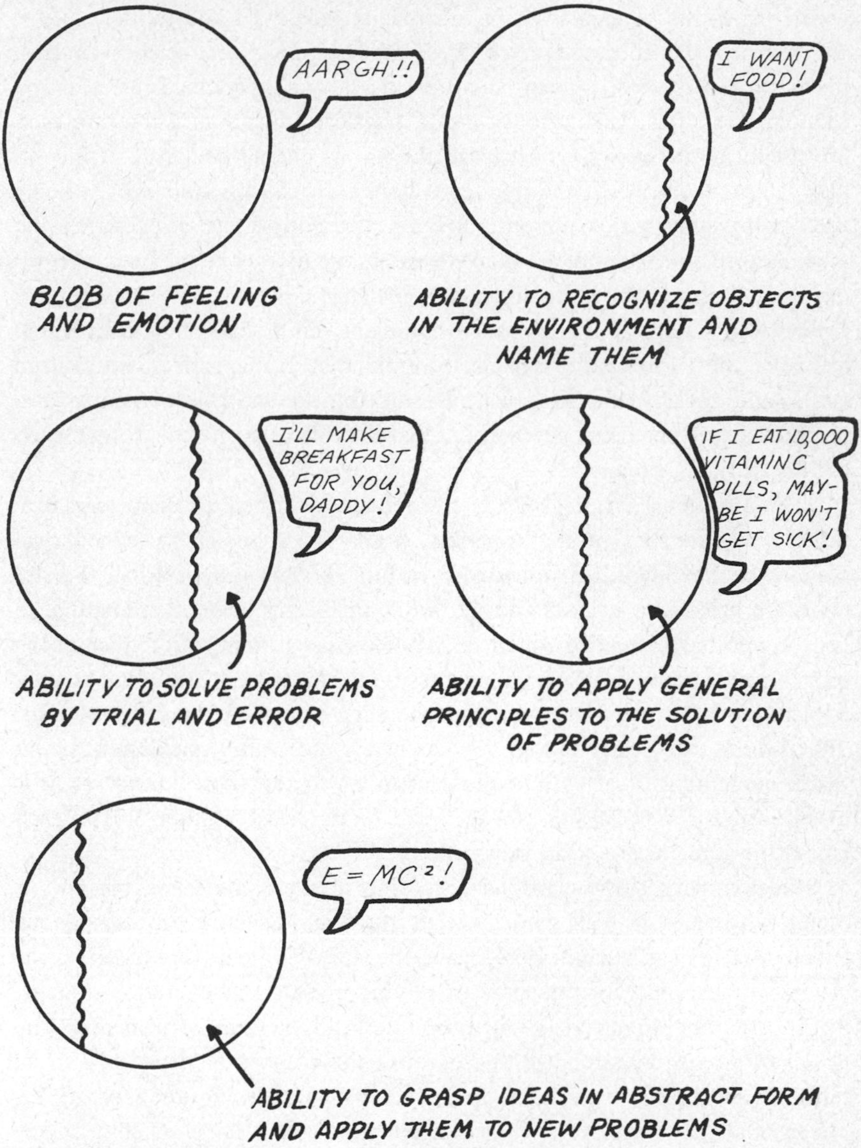

of the teaching of a particular class to a single person. In the primary school the child is learning how to communicate. In the secondary school the adolescent is learning how to use and appreciate the various specialized aspects of modern culture. Thus, in the modern high school there are shop courses, which teach the elements of major skilled trades, art and music courses, which teach the appreciation of these aspects of culture, science courses, social studies courses, foreign language courses, mathematics courses, home economics courses, health courses, and physical education. There are even driver-education courses, which teach the use of one particular, though complex, cultural object. In the primary school each child is guided by a single adult who takes major responsibility for the educational process. In the secondary school the adolescent moves from one teacher to the next, according to speciality. This is a striking acknowledgment that the adolescent has entered a new stage of intellectual development, and social competence. Intellectually, the adolescent is capable of looking at problems from specialized views, and socially the adolescent is able to take the role of people in a position, like a chemistry teacher, not just the role of a particular other, such as "my fifth-grade teacher."

The educational sociologist C. E. Bidwell has described the major organizational characteristics of the American primary and secondary educational system. He has identified four major features of this system. First, the students are broken up according to age. While this seems obvious and natural to people who have attended American schools during their youth, it is not the only possible way of organizing or classifying students. It would be equally possible to classify students according to their scores on standardized tests. This is done to a degree in high schools where there are "track" systems, in which students are placed in courses according to test scores. However, it is normal for the track system to be based on age classification. Within each course the students are of the same age.

Students can also be classified according to their interests. This, too, is done to a degree in high schools where there are "elective" courses among which students can choose. Here, again, the electives are usually based on age classification. Some consequences of relying upon classification of students by age are not immediately obvious. First, this system may increase the power of groups based on age to determine the content of the child's social self. Grading by age may intensify the separate youth culture. Second, this system may take away from the child the experiences that he could gain in associating with younger and older children.

The second major organizational characteristic of the American primary and secondary educational system is contractual hiring of licensed professionals. Teaching is done by people who have gained a certain degree of educational experience, who have shown a certain level of ability, and who have been licensed by state agencies. These people are paid a salary to teach and do not own their offices. This aspect of the American educational system leads to its third characteristic, the combination of bureaucracy and looseness of structure.

The system is bureaucratic because people are hired to perform specific tasks on the basis of attaining certain achievements. The system is loose because the people hired to do the teaching are less controlled from above than most bureaucratic workers. Teachers are considered professionals, capable of taking a large role in determining how to carry out their duties and how to judge whether or not these duties have been done in a satisfactory manner. While it is possible to judge many bureaucratic personnel on the basis of the amount of acceptable work they do, this is much more difficult with teachers. The test scores that students attain is one measure of teacher effectiveness that is used in some schools as a means for controlling the activity of teachers. There is no universal agreement that this measure is valid. Thus, schools are looser than many other bureaucratic organizations, because the teacher is given some range in decision making. Like grading by age, bureaucratization and professionalization have consequences that are not obvious. Both processes may hinder experimentation with new methods out of fear that organizational expectations will be disturbed and out of the limitations and biases of professional education. Also, both processes may make school and teacher ill-equipped to adapt to students with varying cultural backgrounds.

The fourth characteristic of the American primary and secondary educational system is that the school is responsible both to its students and to interest groups within the community. This double responsibility creates difficult problems and conflicts. Within the American idea of democratic education is the notion that the schools should respond to the needs of communities. Local schools in the United States have frequently adapted their course offerings to fit the requirements of industries in the community for certain kinds of skilled labor. Schools have also offered foreign languages of interest to members of ethnic groups within the community. They have used materials and brought in lecturers supplied by patriotic, business, labor, veterans, and other interest groups. They have run ambitious athletic programs to satisfy spectators within the community. They have offered special history courses to meet the demands of elements in the community, as in the case of black history being offered in many black neighborhood schools. However, also within the idea of American education in a democracy is the notion that the best instruction should be provided by competent professionals who are responsible for the intellectual development of their students. The two notions of responsiveness to community and professional responsibility have often clashed. Today the issue is usually joined in the debate over local control of schools. In some neighborhoods, both black and white, parents and interest groups have demanded wide control over who is hired to teach, which children are allowed to enter the school, and what is taught. These kinds of demands are not new in American history and they illustrate the continuing interplay between responsiveness to community and professional responsibility. It is too easy to say that the administration and activities of the schools should be left to professional teachers. Much of the liveliness in American education has stemmed from community involvement in the schools. Such involvement ranges from debates over the size and content of the school budget to the nature of the courses offered.

DILEMMAS OF EDUCATION

The American public school, as an organization which classifies students by age, hires licensed professionals, runs with a combination of bureaucracy and structural looseness, and has dual professional and community responsibilities, wields a profound impact on the development of the children and adolescents who attend it. The staff at each school generally holds an interpretation of the roles of student and child that will affect the intellectual and social development of the students. This impact occurs in several ways. First, the staff has an interpretation of what constitutes a good student. Historically, the good student has been seen as one who is obedient, diligent, quiet, and clean. Students who had these characteristics were rewarded and those who did not were not given praise and high grades. This meant that middle-class children thrived more than those of lower classes in the system, and at least in early grades, girls were more likely to adapt to school than boys. The child who does not or cannot play the role of good student is likely to be frustrated and, perhaps, to feel inadequate.

The second way in which the school makes an impact on social development is by classifying some children as capable of being good students and others as incapable of educational development. Here, the staff may consider students incapable of learning because they have a certain skin color or belong to a certain religious or national group. In this case, the students in the less favored group are highly unlikely to achieve educational success. The two ways in which the school has an impact on the intellectual and social development of the child point to some conclusions about academic achievement. Students may lack the motivation to achieve because they come from backgrounds in which they have not been encouraged to learn the role of good student. They may also lack the desire to achieve because the staff of the school believes them to be incapable of excellence. In either case it is clear that achievement and motivation are not merely problems of the individual, but are part of complex social processes.

HIGHER EDUCATION

The same factors that were responsible for the growth of the primary school and later for the growth of the secondary school have worked to create in the United States a vast system of post-adolescent education composed of junior colleges, colleges, universities, and professional schools. The prime causes for this growth have been the increase in jobs demanding ever greater skill with complex symbol systems and tools, the demand by people that their children have the education necessary to fill these jobs, and the judgment that higher education will allow one to appreciate contemporary culture. While American institutions of higher education are less age graded than primary and secondary schools, they share with the primary and secondary schools bureaucratization, professionalism, and a two-sided commitment to students and groups within the community. They began as organizations for training ministers, school teachers, and sometimes other professionals like lawyers and doctors. They have become the major instruments for developing talent to run the specialized processes characteristic of contemporary life.

Institutions of higher education are faced with much the same dilemma as are primary and secondary schools. There are responsibilities both to the students and to the community. This dilemma is at the heart of current campus unrest and student movements for reform of higher education and social change. Those students who disagree with the present organization of higher education make two major claims. First, they say that the institutions of higher education are emphasizing services to the community and groups within it more than they are concentrating on teaching students. This is the argument which says that professors should spend more time teaching and less time in research and consulting. It also states that institutions should provide more facilities for students and less for interest groups within the community. This aspect of the student movement at universities has had the effect of arousing new interest in teaching at these institutions. Junior colleges and community colleges have mainly concentrated on teaching from their beginnings.

The second claim of the students who disagree with the present organization of higher education is that the junior colleges, colleges, and universities are providing service to the wrong groups and withholding service from the right groups. In this case, some spokesmen for the student movement argue that most of the research and service carried out by institutions of higher education benefits well-established bureaucracies, such as those concerned with military affairs, manufacturing, commerce, and government administration. They claim that relatively little research and service goes to groups such as the poor who have been left out of the mainstream of bureaucratized society, and to projects such as pollution control. These two claims—that universities stress research and service to groups within the community over teaching, and that higher education emphasizes service to some groups rather than others—have caused a large amount of current campus unrest and a reason for student movements for social change. These claims and the movements that stem from them are intertwined with the central problem of American institutions of higher education and other American schools, the interplay of responsibility to students and responsibility to groups within the community. In the universities, colleges, and junior colleges this problem is complicated by the demands of some students for greater control over their living conditions and the form and content of their education. It is likely that these issues will continue to be important in the foreseeable future.

THE MASS COMMUNICATIONS MEDIA

In the contemporary world education is not confined to the school or college. Much of the information that people receive about role definitions, how to use products, what styles of life are available, what goes on in other cultures, how to avoid dangers around them, and what political decisions affect them, is communicated through the mass media of communication: newspapers, magazines, movies, radio, television. Like educational institutions, the mass media grew up as roles became more specialized; new technologies such as movable type, the vacuum tube, and transistors were developed; and a mass market developed for products. Media of communication extend the human senses. For example, newspapers extend the eye by allowing the person to find out about human events far removed from his physical surroundings. Radio extends the ear in the same way. Television extends both eye and ear, and may involve other senses substitutionally, such as touch.

Through media various messages are transmitted. However, communications analyst Marshall McLuhan points out that the medium and the message should not be completely divorced. By involving different senses, different media give rise to different experiences. McLuhan believes that for most of the modern age print was the dominant mass medium. He states that print isolates a person from others and makes him an observer with a point of view. He continues that in the present post-modern era of electronic media, people around the world are involved with one another immediately and can no longer take the role of observer, whether passionate or dispassionate. For this reason, he claims that post-modern human beings are becoming retribalized (regrouped) and will no longer agree to play standardized, bureaucratic roles.

Many communications analysts do not go as far as McLuhan, but they still argue that the media are very important factors in the contemporary educational process. The mass media are important because they reach very large groups of people with the same message. It becomes a significant task for social scientists to determine what groups control the messages that are carried on the media and what principles they use to select these messages. In dictatorships all of the mass media are closely controlled by the dominant political party. In contemporary representative democracies, selling products is an important deciding factor of media content. In the West, however, journalists have professional standing and, therefore, there is a large degree of independence in reporting the news. In this respect the mass media are somewhat similar to the schools. They are both bureaucratized and, in some aspects, professionalized. In the contemporary world they form a second school system.

SUMMARY

Communication is the transfer of information about cultural objects and other aspects of the world from one person to another. The process of education is a type of communications process in which the person learns how to use, appreciate, and organize cultural objects such as tools, products, rules, and symbols. Education is a developmental process which parallels the development of the social self and mature individual.

In the first stage of intellectual development the child learns by trial and error and is capable of naming the objects around him according to the sense qualities that they display. He can identify his toy truck. In the second stage of intellectual development the child can use general principles to solve concrete problems without fully understanding these principles in their abstract statement. He can repair his toy truck when the wheels fall off, even if he does not know why the wheels fell off. In the third stage of intellectual development the adolescent becomes able to grasp principles as general ideas and to apply them in new circumstances. He can understand that a wheel makes travel from one place to another more efficient. These three stages correspond respectively to expressing wants, taking the role of particular others, and taking the role of general others.

The school is the center for education in the modern age. Primary schools arose to teach children means of communication such as reading, writing, and counting which their parents were not equipped to teach. Secondary schools and colleges grew up to teach large numbers of people the new skills, symbol systems, and roles required by a highly specialized culture in contact with many other cultures. Similarly, the mass media of communication have knit together people in this specialized culture.

Much education in present-day life still takes place in the family, community, and religious organizations. However, these units of life have become largely devoted to the appreciation and enjoyment of culture. The next chapter will show how the processes of economics, politics, and education find their fulfillment in the process of appreciation.

Notes

[1] Jerome S. Bruner, *The Process of Education* (New York: Vintage Books, 1960), p. 34.

[2] Bruner, *The Process of Education*, p. 34.

[3] Bruner, *The Process of Education*, p. 37-38.

Suggested Readings

Boorstin, D. *The Image: A Guide to Pseudo-Events in America*, New York: Harper & Row, Publishers, 1961 (paper).

Bruner, J. S. *The Process of Education*, New York: Random House, Inc., 1960 (paper).

Coleman, J. S. *The Adolescent Society*, New York: The Free Press, 1961.

Conant, J. *American High School Today*, New York: McGraw-Hill Book Company, 1959 (paper).

Dewey, J. *Democracy and Education*, New York: The Macmillan Company, 1961 (paper).

Goslin, D. A. *A School in Contemporary Society*, Glenview: Scott, Foresman and Company, 1965 (paper).

Hollingshead, A. B. *Elmstown's Youth*, New York: John Wiley & Sons, Inc., 1949 (paper).

Jencks, C. and Riesman, D. *The Academic Revolution*, Garden City: Doubleday & Company, Inc., 1968.

Kenniston, K. *The Uncommitted: Alienated Youth in American Society*, New York: Dell Publishing Co., Inc., 1960 (paper).

Kozol, J. *Death at an Early Age: The Destruction of the Hearts and Minds of Negro Children in the Boston Public Schools*, Boston: Houghton Mifflin Company, 1967.

Larsen, O. N. *Violence and the Mass Media*, New York: Harper & Row, Publishers, 1968 (paper).

McLuhan, M. *Understanding Media: The Extensions of Man*, New York: New American Library of World Literature, Inc., 1964 (paper).

Neill, A. S. *Summerhill*, New York: Hart Publishing Co., Inc., 1960.

Piaget, J. *The Moral Judgment of the Child*, New York: The Free Press, 1962 (paper).

Skinner, B. F. *Walden Two*, New York: The Macmillan Company, 1960 (paper).

von Hoffman, N. *The Multiversity: A Personal Report on What Happens to Today's Students at American Universities*, New York: Holt, Rinehart & Winston, Inc., 1966.

CHAPTER EIGHT: SOCIAL ROLES AND PROCESSES

By themselves, the processes of creating, preserving, destroying, and distributing culture (economics), coordinating the uses of culture (politics), and learning about culture (education) have no complete meaning. Culture is produced, coordinated, and taught so that it can be used, appreciated, and enjoyed. The major settings in which the *appreciation* of culture occurs are the family, the community, and religious organizations. In each of these settings culture is used to cement relationships among people both so that they will be able to perform their roles in other social processes and so that they will gain certain ultimate values in their existence. The love and respect that characterize family life at its best, the friendship and solidarity that mark strong communities, and the brotherhood and concern shown by tightly knit religious associations are some of the values possible in the major settings for cultural appreciation. That these values are not always present is a fact obvious to most human beings. However, it is doubtful that in any group of human beings which has all of the four major social processes these values will be lacking completely. The motivation necessary for performing one's social roles is derived largely from the support given by people to one another in family, community, and religious associations; and on the significant and highly valued experiences obtained by the individual in these associations.

The appreciative institutions—family, community, and religion—are founded on different principles from those underlying economic, political, and educational institutions. Economic institutions are concerned with the allocation of scarce resources to the various human activities. Political institutions are concerned with coordinating these activities, or keeping them from interfering with one another. Educational institutions are concerned with transmitting information about human activities from some people to others. The family, community, and religion function to make the activity in the other institutions meaningful to the individual. The family is the central point at which the economic activity of the individual becomes meaningful in the use of culture and its enjoyment in the company of others. The community is the central point at which the political activity of the individual becomes meaningful in a pattern of public life. It can be visibly experienced in public buildings and public services, and internally experienced as a spirit of community pride and high morale, or community shame and dissension. The religious association is the central point at which the educational activity of the individual and his experience throughout the social processes become meaningful. He learns the final purpose of human existence and feels a group experience of dedication to this purpose. Thus, the family, the community, and religion are the settings in which the activities and products of the other social processes are appreciated and related to one another in patterns of private and public life.

SOCIAL MAN

Sociologists who have studied the family, community, and religion, have frequently used a model of the human being different from that used by economists, political scientists, and educators. Economic man, as described by economists, is a person devoted to satisfying desires which he has arranged in a scale of preference. He seeks satisfaction rationally, acquiring information about the cheapest and surest means to his ends and acting on this information to gain maximum satisfaction. He takes for granted a world in which he is free to gain information about the nature of his desires, the means of attaining his goals, and the role expectations connected with different tasks. Economic man is a model, not a role that people actually perform (although some people try to become economic men). All of the things that economic man takes for granted are investigated carefully by political scientists. Political man, as described by political scientists, is a being devoted to gaining the conditions necessary for him to satisfy any of his desires. When there is no coordination among human activities and no enforcement of the most important role obligations, there is a war of all against all. Political man lives in constant fear that expectations will not be fulfilled and that he will be subject to attack on his life and property. He seeks the power necessary to prevent such attack. Like economic man, political man is a model to which few people even attempt to conform. While political man takes less for granted than economic man, he still assumes that people have learned how to recognize valuable property and that they have the skills necessary to seize it and use it. This knowledge, taken for granted by political man, is investigated carefully by the student of education.

The student of education, too, has a model of man that he works with for purposes of analysis. This role defines the human being as someone with very general drives, who is taught a cultural system. The learning process goes through stages beginning with trial and error problem solving and ending with systematic application of general principles to particular situations. Like the models of economic man and political man, this model also contains unexamined assumptions.

Before education occurs there must be a social relationship. The roles of economic man, political man, and learning man are filled out by the role of social man. *Social man* acts to gain the approval of those around him. While economic man is interested in acquiring the things that will satisfy his desires, social man is concerned with creating favorable impressions in the minds of others. It is social man who is at the root of the question, "What will people think if I do this?" This question can have two meanings. First, a person can ask it with the intent of finding out what to expect from others if he undertakes a certain course of action. In this case he may or may not care about whether the others will approve of the action. He is only concerned with predicting what they will do when he acts. A son may take his father's attitudes into account before he joins a political movement, not because he seeks approval, but because he wants continued financial support. Second, a person can ask the question with the intent of finding out what the others will think if he performs the action so that he can pattern his activity to win their approval.

In the first case, a person might predict that others would find it distasteful if he stood up his date. He might then go ahead and stand her up because he did not expect them to take any outward action against him. In the second case, if he predicted that they would find his conduct distasteful and would disapprove of it, he would not stand up his date. Social man not only takes the role of the other, he takes the role of the other so that he can pattern his own actions after the other's expectations. Philosopher William James remarked that the most powerful motivation for human beings was neither wealth, power, nor knowledge, but the presence of favorable ideas about themselves in the minds of other human beings. This led James to say that an individual's social self was contained in the minds of other people. Dependent in such an important way on the judgments of others, social man provides the bonds that make economic man, political man, and learning man possible. Yet social man is also a model. Few, if any, people spend their whole lives attempting only to win approval.

PRIMARY GROUPS

Social man, the appreciator of culture, who is nourished by others and nourishes them in turn, is formed in primary groups. Sociologist Charles Horton Cooley defined the term *primary group*: "By primary groups I mean those characterized by intimate face-to-face association and cooperation. They are primary in several senses, but chiefly in that they are fundamental in forming the social nature and ideas of the individual. The result of intimate association, psychologically, is a certain fusion of individualities in a common whole, so that one's very self, for many purposes at least, is the common life and purpose of the group."[1] Thus, primary groups are quite different from the corporations, labor unions, political regimes, bureaucracies, schools, and mass communications systems discussed under the headings of economic, political, and educational processes.

Organizations like corporations are secondary groups, bringing together more people than can unite on a face-to-face basis. Within corporations and other bureaucratic organizations there are many primary groups composed of co-workers in close contact with one another. They are the creators of the web of informal organization that grows up within any formal organization. For example, roommates in a dormitory form a primary group. However, despite the appearance of primary groups within the boundaries of secondary groups, the most important primary group is the family. It is in the family that there is a maximum of face-to-face association and cooperation. It is also

MORE OF THE SELF IS INVOLVED IN A PRIMARY GROUP THAN IN A SECONDARY GROUP

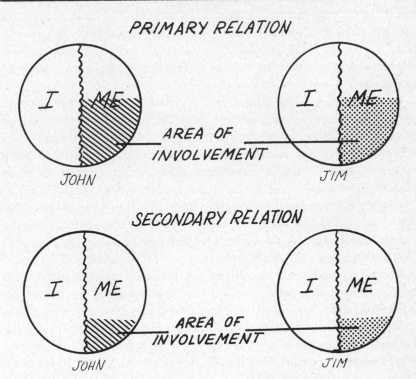

PRIMARY RELATION

I   ME   AREA OF INVOLVEMENT

JOHN   JIM

SECONDARY RELATION

I   ME   AREA OF INVOLVEMENT

JOHN   JIM

in the family that the social self, or "me," is developed through the process of taking the roles first of particular others and later of others in social positions. The primary group is the center of the process of appreciation and the family is the most important primary group.

THE FAMILY

Historically, the family has been thought of as the primary social institution. In its basic and normal form in present-day Western societies, the *family* is made up of a husband and wife, and children to whom they are biological parents. This pattern, although it is the one that springs to mind when the word *family* is mentioned, frequently is not fulfilled in actual families. First, the children may not be related biologically to the parents. The children may be adopted, or one of the parents may be a stepparent. In this case, the husband and wife take the social role of parents towards the children, even though they are not biologically related. Second, there may only be one parent living with the children. This condition may arise from the death of one of the marriage partners, or divorce or separation. The family made up of a husband and wife, and children to whom they are biologically related is called the *nuclear family*. While the nuclear family is considered as the measure for family life in the West, it is not necessarily the best or most "natural" arrangement.

Beyond changes in the nuclear family pattern brought on by adoption, remarriage, divorce, or death of one parent, the nuclear family itself can be compared with the extended family. The *extended family* is composed of a number of biologically related people and their nuclear families. Before the modern era and the rise of corporations, labor unions, bureaucracies, and mass communications, most people lived their lives within extended families. The family would extend in time over more than two generations and in space over more than a single unit of parents and children. Often, where the extended family appears, the mother's brother, not the father, takes responsibility for bringing up the children.

Whether the person is brought up in a nuclear family or an extended family will have important results for the development of the self. In the progression of self development the human being goes from expressing desires to taking the role of particular others, to taking the role of others in social positions, to taking the role of human being in his culture. The deciding stage in self development comes when the child begins to take the role of particular others. In the extended family there are many people whose thoughts, feelings, and actions must be taken into account when deciding upon a plan of action. The child in an extended family must ask what many particular others would think if he performed a given action. This means that no one person is likely to exercise a crucial influence on the development of the social self, or "me." It also means that there is not likely to be great differences between the social selves of people within the group. They will have all taken the roles of the same people (particular others) and will have taken the roles of one another.

The very opposite of the situation in the extended family occurs in the nuclear family. Here, the child takes the roles of very few particular others, perhaps only his mother and father. This means that the mother and father have a very significant influence on the development of the social self. It also means that individual differences among parents will tend to be exaggerated. This fact led the psychiatrist Sigmund Freud to believe that events in the first few years of a person's life are decisive for his future development. While there is disagreement about how important parental impact is on the child's development, there is no doubt that in the nuclear family parents play a large role in shaping the expectations of the developing social self. This puts a huge burden of responsibility on parents in contemporary Western societies, which often leads to guilt, despair, and attempts to deny the responsibility.

Sociologist John Sirjamaki has identified eight dominant characteristics of the contemporary American nuclear family. First, a lasting and happy marriage is a key goal in life for both men and women. Marriage is seen as the proper way for discharging sexual impulses, satisfying emotional needs, and procreating children. The single adult is viewed as somehow abnormal and approximately 92 percent of adults have been married at least once by the time they reach the age of sixty-five. Second, marriage should be based on personal affection and voluntary choice. Although many people may get married because they want to gain social mobility, wealth, or approval of their parents, Americans are supposed to marry for love. Men assume that the decision to marry is their own, and women are dependent upon a proposal This inequality, which makes women compete with one another in a marriage market, has been challenged by the current movement for female equality. The idea that marriages should be based on romantic love puts great strains on the husband and wife when they experience specific problems of adjusting conflicting role expectations. Third, Americans judge whether or not their marriage is successful by whether they are personally happy. Generally they believe that happiness is dependent upon having children and that remaining childless is selfish. They also believe that if they are not happy, or if their initial romantic love fades, the marriage should be ended. In most cultures love is not viewed as important in marriage. The assumption is that any two normal people can build a satisfactory married life. Perhaps the personal differences encouraged in the nuclear family account for the importance of romantic love in the West. Where extended families are dominant, exactly who the marriage partner is may not be as important.

The fourth characteristic of the American nuclear family is the high value put on youth. Youth is regarded as a period of innocence and energy. This view differs from the situation in cultures such as the Chinese, in which age is valued as an indication of experience and youth is looked upon as a period of immaturity. The high value put on youth in America may cause resentment in middle-aged people and may partly account for the generation gap. Fifth, Americans believe that children should be raised in a world of their own, apart from adult responsibilities and problems. The idea is that children should be shielded from tragedy and allowed to grow up in toyland. This sheltering, especially in the middle class, may also be partly responsible for the generation gap, because many people are shocked when they are suddenly introduced to the adult world in late adolescence. Sixth, Americans believe that sexual activity should be confined to marital relations. While this belief is not always realized in action, it creates guilt in those who break the rule.

The seventh characteristic of the American nuclear family is the belief that the roles of husband and wife should be based on a sexual division of labor with the husband as head of the family, breadwinner and representative in the community, and the wife as homemaker. This belief also creates tension, because many women provide income for the household and have come to demand equality in treatment. This aspect of the American family is fast becoming a myth with little basis in practice. Eighth, the American family is supposed to exist for the benefit of its individual members. This sums up the other characteristics and shows the strains under which the American family labors. Concentration on individual satisfaction weakens the unity of the family and divides the individual's loyalties between his roles within the family and his roles outside. The American family has great difficulty competing with the powerful and bureaucratized economic, political, educational, and community organizations surrounding it. Based on individualism, it tends to dissolve when opportunities call individuals to other sectors of the social process.

Over the years, the family in the West has progressively lost its major functions. In the Middle Ages it was the primary unit of economic production, education, appreciation, and socialization. It was also the link of the individual to the political system and the key element in religious practice. Today it has lost its economic dominance to the corporation and the labor union, its educational dominance to the school and mass media, its political dominance to the party and interest group, and its religious dominance to the individual conscience and other social groupings. It keeps the function of socializing the infant and shares the function of appreciation with clubs and entertainment institutions. Its most important present-day function is providing a setting in which people can take part in close primary relations. Whether it can perform this function well, considering the strains under which it works, is a question which can only be answered by future developments.

COMMUNITY

Beyond the family is the community. As in the case of the family, there is no single satisfactory definition of the community. Sociologist Morris Ginsberg defined the *community* as "a group of social beings living a common life, including all the infinite variety and complexity of relations which result from that common life or constitute it."[2] This definition describes what people usually refer to when they use the word *community*. Community is thought of as an encompassing organization of human beings, located in a particular area, and containing both formal and informal social relations. In addition, people think that members of a community are knit together by a common attachment to their way of life and to one another. This view of community defines a pattern of human existence that is frequently not realized in contemporary Western life. In urban communities, like New York City, Chicago, and any other metropolis, the bonds of common life are frequently stretched thin and the boundaries of the community ("Chicagoland" or the "New York Metropolitan Area") are vague and extended in space. Important activities of community members are performed outside of community boundaries, many people do not have a positive feeling about city life, and there is often little solidarity among members. Yet people consider the close-knit community as the normal pattern and view the urban community as different from it. This points up the bias against urban life present in American attitudes. It does not make urban life any less the major setting for the appreciation of culture beyond the family.

The definition of a community as a number of people sharing a common life in a well defined area applies best to agricultural communities. Just as there were important differences between the extended family and the nuclear family, there are significant differences between the rural community and the urban community. These differences have importance in the development of the human self.

In the *rural community* there are relatively few economic, political and educational roles, and those roles that do exist are relatively unspecialized and well known to the members of the community. Thus, in the rural community it is easy for people to take the roles of others. *People tend to reveal only those aspects of themselves that others are likely to understand*. This means that in the rural community people tend to reveal large parts of themselves to others. There is little privacy in the rural community, not only because of prying and gossip by neighbors, but because people are not widely different from one another. Each person has taken the same roles in the process of developing his social self and, therefore, is much like the others in his judgments about expected behaviors. In a close-knit and relatively isolated rural community, a person can make quite accurate guesses about what others are doing and thinking because he carries the community within himself. The others are likely to be doing and thinking just what he is. In exchange for this loss of privacy the member of the rural community gains a large amount of stability in his social existence. He can count on role expectations being met. Since this stability can be shattered easily by the introduction of new elements, members of rural communities tend to distrust strangers and to resist adding new tools, products, symbols, and rules to their common life.

The *urban community* is the very opposite of the rural community. It is based on the intense specialization that has occurred with the rise of corporations, labor unions, democratic regimes, bureaucracies, schools, and mass media of communication. Urban communities are large in size, population, and density of population. Most importantly, they combine intense specialization with wide cultural differences. If people tend to reveal only those parts of themselves that others are likely to understand, members of urban communities reveal very little of themselves to most others. Any particular urban dweller is not likely to have taken many of the roles present in his community. He may not understand the roles of specialists such as nuclear engineers, sociologists, brain surgeons, actuaries, and many others. He may not understand even the roles of human being present in groups such as American Indians, blacks, Chinese Americans, and Mexican Americans. Thus, the urban dweller can count much less on the fulfillment of his expectations than his rural counterpart. He is in the difficult position of having to trust others at the very time that he has little reason to trust them. The mass media ease this situation somewhat by informing urban dwellers of the different role definitions present in the community. They will run stories on the activities of specialists and the hopes of cultural groups. The schools also provide such information. However, this second-hand information is a poor substitute for the first-hand knowledge that the rural person has. The urban dweller cannot gain a good idea of what others are doing and thinking by looking at himself. His experiences are far different from those of many others.

The uncertainty of the urban dweller is greatly reduced in two ways. First, urban communities are broken up into neighborhoods in which similar kinds of people live. These neighborhoods resemble in some respects rural communities. They are villages within a wider urban setting. Within the neighborhoods there are often close primary group relationships and high morale. Within the neighborhood there are fewer roles than within the wider community, and there is frequently one dominant cultural group. Thus, in the neighborhood people recreate some of the stability present in the rural community.

SELVES IN RURAL AND URBAN AREAS

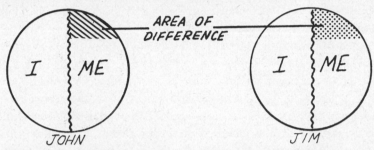

SOCIAL SELVES ARE SIMILAR IN RURAL AREAS

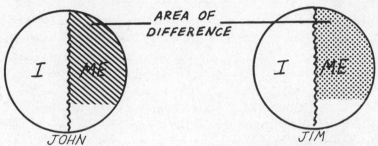

SOCIAL SELVES ARE DIFFERENT IN URBAN AREAS

Similar to the neighborhood is the homogeneous (made up of the same kind) suburb, populated by people with similar incomes and life styles. Both the neighborhood and the suburb show that many people do not like the impersonality of urban life and yearn for the stability and close ties of the rural community. This may be one of the major reasons many neighborhoods and suburbs resemble rural communities in their dread of strangers (fear of blacks moving into white neighborhoods and suburbs), and in their resistance to new symbols (fear of educational experiments in many suburbs). However, neighborhoods and suburbs are not like rural communities in all respects. They are quite open to new products and tools. They sometimes resist new rules that threaten their way of life, but they sometimes press for new rules that will provide them with greater services. In the neighborhood and suburb many people find a setting for the appreciation of culture.

The second way in which the urbanite's uncertainty is reduced is by the presence of a special code governing urban life. This code cuts through to the common trait of all the specialized and different cultural roles, and expresses a stripped-down role of the human being. This stripped-down role of human being includes a principle of live and let live, and noninterference. The person is expected to perform his specialized duties and to allow others to carry out their obligations. He is not supposed to interfere in the affairs of others. In a striking phrase, these affairs are "none of his business." On the streets, in parks, in public buildings, and on public transportation, the person is expected to keep to himself. He is not supposed to bother strangers with his problems, strike up conversations with them, or intrude in other ways on their privacy. There are exceptions to this rule in the case of people who need directions. Specialists are supposed to handle problems, leaving others free to follow their daily plans relatively unburdened. This stripped-down role of human being and live and let live ethic is responsible for the supposed coldness of city life. However, it is probably necessary to allow people enough freedom and privacy to conduct their affairs. The live and let live ethic of urban life does not include the rule that one should not get involved even when terrible crimes are being committed or people are on the verge of death. This perversion is more an ethic of live and let die.

The urban community, which is bound together by neighborhoods and the stripped-down role of human being, has always been a center of cultural conflict and such problems as congestion, deteriorating housing, environmental pollution, and crime (although the percentage of violent crimes is higher in rural areas, and rural dwellers have worse medical care and often worse housing than urbanites). However, the city has also been the setting for the expansion of human freedom and culture. The urbanite, who dreams of returning to the land, frequently wants to take the conveniences of city life along with him.

RELIGION

Beyond both family and community, religion is the final setting for human appreciation. *Religions* are systems of belief, ritual, organization, ethics, and emotion that link human beings to their environments. As systems of belief, religions provide accounts of the ultimate nature of the universe, the place of human beings and communities within that universe, and the final purposes of human existence. They offer explanations of why evil occurs in the world and state what meanings a person can attach to his own death and the death of others.

As systems of ritual, religions provide means through which human beings and communities keep contact with a supposed area of existence beyond that known to the senses. Through ritual, human beings believe that they participate in a reality beyond this world and keep the favor of powers that control vital earthly events. They communicate with their gods. In many communities, particularly among preliterate peoples, members believe that if rituals are not performed correctly the gods will take vengeance upon the entire community. This belief was used to justify human sacrifice among the Aztec Indians of preconquest Mexico. In the West, where individual and community salvation are not so closely bound, ritual is relatively less important than it is elsewhere. Historically, ritual has been an important way of maintaining the bonds of community, because it brings people together in a common experience that they believe is of decisive importance to the welfare of the whole.

As systems of organization, religions provide the means of standardizing the ultimate relations of human beings to their environments. Such problems as determining the final purposes of human existence and the place of human beings within the universe are open to many possible and conflicting answers. Religious organizations play an important part in the process of socialization because they offer solutions for such problems. Further, religious organizations provide a setting in which people can renew their social bonds with one another and can rededicate themselves to more cooperative relationships.

As systems of ethics, religions provide the definition of the role of human being in most groups. It is the religions of the world that have provided the most influential conceptions of the role of human being. These conceptions have been far richer than others that have seemed to characterize different phases of the social process. Economic man, who acts to get the most satisfaction of his demands; political man, who acts to gain the conditions for attaining some of his aspirations; learning man, who comes to know a cultural system; and social man, who seeks the approval of others, are far more specialized concepts than the creative human being described by some of the world religions. In some religious views the creative "I" does not stand apart from the social "me," but becomes the fulfillment of the social "me."

As systems of feeling or emotion, religions organize the emotional lives of human beings around stable sets of objects, experiences, and actions. Feelings such as piety, mystery, loss of self in a larger whole, and ecstasy can be attached to a wide variety of objects and actions. Religions channel these feelings and emotions into support for ethical systems, particular organizations, rituals, and beliefs. In ordering the emotional lives of human beings, religions perform their primary function as appreciative institutions. When his deepest feelings are given some meaning in a collective life, the person is fit to appreciate other aspects of culture and his fellow human beings. However, religion does not always enable the person to accept better the other aspects of his culture. The role of human being offered by religion may separate from the role requirements of more specialized activities. In this case there is tension between religion and other aspects of human existence such as economics, politics, and education. Such tension is illustrated by the debates about whether one can be successful in business and fulfill religious obligations, whether one can lead a religious life and go to war, and whether one can explore rationally the structure of the world and maintain religious beliefs.

The role of human being most common in the West is that defined in the Judaeo-Christian religious tradition. In this tradition the human being is viewed as a creature marked by insistent desires who is capable of overcoming these desires and of loving others and God. The human being is supposed to have an immortal soul, and his time on earth is supposed to be a trial period before a final judgment on the fate of his soul. To aid the salvation of his soul he is supposed to follow certain commandments. In Judaism these commandments are contained in the Decalogue and in Christianity they are summed up in the moral law, "Love thy neighbor as thyself." Thus, the Judaeo-Christian tradition claims that the human being has a dual nature. The person is subject to greed and selfish desire, but is also capable of aiding others. Since each person is viewed as having this possibility for goodness, Judaeo-Christian thought has often emphasized the idea that each individual has an inner worth and dignity. This idea has been important in humanitarian movements, democratic revolutions, and movements for social equality.

Another aspect of Judaeo-Christian thought which has had profound impact on social processes in the West is its philosophy of history. Both Jews and Christians believe in a historical religion in which a drama of salvation unfolds. After man's fall from grace, there is a period of waiting for the coming of a savior. For Jews, the Savior has not yet come. For Christians, He has come as Christ and will come again, and He has instituted a new law which goes beyond that of the Old Testament. This view of history contrasts with that of other religions, such as the Hindu faith, in which history is seen as an endless cycle of death and rebirth. The straight-line, rather than cyclical, view of history in the Judaeo-Christian tradition has influenced both social thought and social action in the West. Periodically, social movements have appeared in the West to prepare for the coming of the Savior or actually to do the work of the Savior by creating heaven on earth through a political and social revolution. Marxism draws upon this pattern, as do all schemes of thought which trace the history of man through a first stage of innocence and bliss, a second stage of toil and conflict, and a third stage of heaven on earth in which conflicts have been solved and human beings are free to seek their dreams in a surrounding of plenty. Through the spread of Christianity and Marxism throughout the world, this idea of history has entered cultures in which it once would never have been understood.

In the United States, a particular pattern of religious life has developed which points out many of the problems of religion in the modern world. For Americans, religion is primarily a matter of individual conscience, and the performance of religious rituals is not tied directly to the survival of the community. Thus, in America church is separated from state. There is no established state religion, as there is in England, Spain, and many other nations. Instead, a large number of churches, sects, denominations, and cults coexist, sometimes in uneasy peace. In this situation religion becomes linked in certain respects to social class. It becomes a badge of one's status in the community. Thus, among Protestants, there are larger proportions of upper- and upper-middle class families which are Episcopalians and Presbyterians than which are Methodists and Baptists. In general, Catholics have lower social rank than Protestants.

Religious life in America has adapted to a mainly secular society in which the leading institutions are corporations, labor unions, administrative organizations, and other bureaucracies. In this adaptation it has lost some of the importance that it had in organizing early American communities, such as the Puritan settlements in New England. Like the family and the close-knit community, religion has been on the defensive in American society. In this context, movements have appeared within the churches for uniting various denominations (ecumenicism) and for making religion more relevant to solving the political, economic, and cultural conflicts of the contemporary world. It is too early to determine whether these movements will be successful in restoring religion to a central place in the appreciative life of human beings.

SUMMARY

In addition to economic man, political man, and learning man, social scientists use the idea of social man to describe aspects of human activity. Rather than seeking maximum gratification of desires, the peace necessary to satisfy any desires at all, or knowledge of nature and culture, social man seeks the approval of others. In seeking approval, or favorable impressions in the minds of others, social man shows how people are tied together into a collective life. The very self of a human being is extended into the minds of others. At the center of the activity of social man is the process of appreciating culture in the company of others. While this process of appreciation is carried on in clubs, among friends, in organizations devoted to entertainment and cultural enrichment, and in places of recreation, the three major institutions of the appreciative life are the family, the community, and religion.

The contemporary family is nuclear. It is composed of one set of parents and their children. In the nuclear family, the development of the child is highly influenced by the parents, because the child first takes the roles of his parents. Along with the nuclear family goes the urban community, in which the uncertainty caused by specialization and cultural meeting is somewhat eased by a code of live and let live. This code strips down the role of human being to its bare essentials. Opposed to the stripped-down role of human being are the roles of human being offered by the world religions which demand love and creativity rather than noninterference and conformity.

In performing their roles, human beings come into relations with one another. These relations—competition, cooperation, conflict, and love—will be discussed in the next chapter.

Notes

[1] Charles Horton Cooley, *Social Organization* (New York: Charles Scribner's Sons, 1909), p. 23.

[2] Morris Ginsberg, *The Psychology of Society* (London: Methuen and Co., Ltd., 1954), p. 120.

Suggested Readings

Baltzell, E. D. *The Protestant Establishment: Aristocracy and Caste in America*, New York: Random House Inc., 1964 (paper).

Gagnon, J. H. and Simon, W. (ed.), *The Sexual Scene*, Chicago: Aldine Publishing Company, 1970 (paper).

Gans, H. *The Urban Villagers*, New York: The Free Press, 1962 (paper).

Herberg, W. *Protestant-Catholic-Jew*, revised edition, Garden City: Doubleday & Company, Inc., 1955 (paper).

Hunt, M. M. *The World of the Formerly Married*, New York: Fawcett World Library, Crest Books, 1967 (paper).

Komarovsky, M. *Blue-Collar Marriage*, New York: Random House, Inc., 1964 (paper).

Nisbet, R. A. *Community and Power*, New York: Oxford University Press, 1962 (paper).

Vidich, A. J. and Bensman, J. *Small Town in Mass Society: Class, Power, and Religion in a Rural Community*, revised edition, Princeton: Princeton University Press, 1968 (paper).

Yinger, J. M. *Sociology Looks at Religion*, London: Macmillan & Co., Ltd., 1961 (paper).

CHAPTER NINE: HUMAN RELATIONS

The social processes involved in economic, political, educational, and appreciative activities all concern the ways in which human beings use culture. Economic processes, centering on the use of tools, are concerned with the creation, preservation, destruction, and distribution of objects of culture. Political processes, centering on the functions of making and applying rules, are bound up with the coordination of the various uses of culture. Educational processes, whose cores are the transmissions of information about culture, are concerned with the act of symbolic communication. Appreciative processes, which are primarily involved with products, center on the enjoyment and ultimate uses of culture. The patterns that these processes take in human groups make up the social organization of those groups. Social organization is culture in action. Thus, from the viewpoint of the anthropologist roles are systems of rights and duties known to a person taking part in a culture. From the perspectives of students of social organization and processes, as from the perspectives of economists, political scientists, students of education, and sociologists, roles are systems of expected behaviors.

The perspectives of the anthropologist and students of social organization do not use up the systematic ways of thinking about the objects, relations, and aspirations of human beings. Underlying both culture and social organization and processes are the basic forms of human relations. Within the social processes of economics, politics, education, and appreciation are the basic human relations of cooperation, competition, conflict, and concord. The functions of producing, coordinating, communicating, and enjoying culture are carried on by human beings engaged in relations of cooperation, competition, conflict, and concord.

The basic human relations can be readily understood by considering the ways in which people can act with reference to their natural environments and cultures, and with reference to one another's plans. In the case of objects in the natural environment and in the culture, human beings can aid one another in fulfilling goals or attempt to gain as large a share as possible of a limited good. When people give aid to one another in seeking a goal, they are taking part in the human relation of *cooperation*. People can cooperate in building a house. When people attempt to secure a scarce good at the expense of others, they are engaged in the human relation of *competition*. People can compete with one another for grades. Cooperation and competition are human relations centered on securing objects. In the case of human plans, people can attempt to prohibit one another from fulfilling plans or to aid one another in fulfilling plans. When people attempt to deprive one another of success, not primarily because they want to gain a desired object, but because they want to defeat one another, they are taking part in the human relation of *conflict*. People can attempt to damage one another's reputations for the sake of hurting one another. When people attempt to aid one another in achieving success, not primarily because they want to gain a desired object, but because they want to help one another, they are engaged in the human relation of *concord*. People can do favors for one another for the sake of one another's happiness. Conflict and concord are human relations centered on securing consequences for people.

The boundary lines between competition and conflict, and cooperation and concord are fuzzy. Actual human relations frequently shift from primary concern with objects to primary concern with people. For example, one can talk about competition for grades when several students attempt to get the highest marks in a course in which grading is done on a curve. Here, the students compete for grades because they gain satisfaction from high marks, or believe that high marks will aid them in future career advancement. However, competition for grades often becomes conflict among students, when students begin to seek high marks to defeat their rivals and see them come out at the bottom. A similar example will illustrate the shift from cooperation to concord. The members of a work group in a factory or office may cooperate with one another in performing their tasks because they have the goal of receiving wages or salaries, or because they believe that the task is worthwhile. Such cooperation becomes concord when these people begin to help one another because they feel respect and affection for one another. Sometimes concord even prevents accomplishing a task, as when workers in a factory restrict their own output to insure that their less productive colleagues will not be penalized by management. However, despite the fact that competition and conflict, and cooperation and concord shade into one another, there are clear examples in human existence of each relation.

Much of the research done in the structure and dynamics of the basic human relations has been conducted in experimental situations. Small groups of people have been brought together by social scientists and have been told to reach a decision on some matter or to perform a task. Social scientists have observed how the decision was reached or how the task was accomplished, with the hope of understanding the cooperative relation. In other cases, people have been brought together by social scientists as opponents in various games, with the purpose of understanding the competitive relation. In still other laboratory situations, people have been brought together by social scientists and presented with situations challenging their usual judgments of fact and value. Social scientists have observed the ways in which they adjust their attitudes and, perhaps, reach some agreement. Such research touches on the problem of understanding the relation of concord.

Unlike the relations of cooperation, competition, and concord, there are few laboratory studies of the conflict relation. It is difficult and, perhaps, unethical for a social scientist to bring people together in a laboratory situation and to get them to try to defeat one another as persons. This fact points to a criticism that has been made against the social scientists, mainly social psychologists, who have studied human relations in the context of experimental small groups. Critics point out that the situations faced by people in ordinary life are often much more important to them than the situations presented by the laboratory investigator. How can research based on the behaviors of experimental subjects, brought together for short periods of time, shed light on the significant relations of ordinary life? A response to this question is that because the groups studied in laboratory situations are brought together for short periods of time in a controlled setting, their behavior may reveal the most basic patterns of human relations. Another criticism, that small group research reveals patterns of behavior based on the roles of human being present in a culture, is more to the point. However, even if some of the results of small group research are bound to particular cultures, the relations explored appear wherever human beings gather.

Underlying the four major types of human relation, is the general relation of association. Anthropology is based on the fundamental fact that human beings create objects that have meaning to them. People create tools, symbols, rules, and products. The study of social organization is based on the fundamental fact that human beings use the objects that they have created in various ways, recognized under the headings of economic, political, educational, and appreciative activities. Similarly, the study of human relations is founded on a basic fact. Here, it is the fact that human beings have the capability of stimulating one another through their actions. While in many species of animals, individual organisms can stimulate one another (a herd of cattle stimulated to stampede by its own noise), human beings have carried interstimulation farther than any other species. Among human beings the mere act of *associating* is engaged in for its own sake. Sociologist Georg Simmel called special attention to sociability, or "association for its own sake and for the delight in association without the restrictions of practical purposes."[1] *Sociability* is closely related to play and can even be thought of as the social form of play. In the relation of sociability, people gain satisfaction simply because they are in the presence of others. Thus, sociability is the relation of association, when association is sought. Association, however, is far wider than sociability and includes all cases in which human beings stimulate one another. Thus, upon association are built up the four major types of human relations: cooperation, competition, conflict, and concord. Each one follows from the basic fact that human beings stimulate one another.

COOPERATION

Cooperation is the human relation in which people aid one another for the purpose of realizing a goal. There are two major types of cooperation, depending upon the relation of the people to the goal. In its central meaning, cooperation is undertaken by people because they all want to see the same goal accomplished. This kind of cooperation is illustrated by a group of people pushing a car to get it started. Their efforts have meaning because they all want the engine to start running. In preliterate societies, much cooperation is of this type. Members of the group cooperate to build canoes, clear fields, or prepare food because these tasks relate to goals shared by all.

In modern societies, a second type of cooperation becomes important. Here, people cooperate to realize a goal that many of them may not even understand by performing specialized roles. They do not necessarily cooperate because they believe that the goal is worthwhile, but do their duties because they will receive some reward unrelated to accomplishing the task. The clearest case of this kind of cooperation is that of the worker in a factory producing part of a product to be assembled miles away. He does not even know what that product will be, but does the job because he receives wages. Cooperation on large-scale projects in the contemporary world is dependent upon the existence of general media of exchange like money, which allow people to work together, whether or not they care about realizing the group goal. Those people who are in charge of the job and are committed to the group or collective goal usually try to persuade the others to value the goal highly, too. Cooperation based on shared goals is thought to be more effective and stable than cooperation based on rewards unrelated to task fulfillment. This may not always be the case, because people strongly committed to the realization of a project may demand a say in how the tasks are carried out and may rebel when they believe that the decision makers are incompetent. Cooperation ranges from the case in which people are fully committed and involved in attaining a goal to the case in which people are not even aware of the goal but fulfill their duties because they will receive a reward for doing so.

Studies of cooperation in experimental groups have concentrated on the relation in which participants want to see the same goal realized. Social scientists have found that when a small group of people is given a task to perform, various members of the group take on different roles. This may mean that certain roles are inseparable from the cooperative relation. The most important roles observed by social scientists are those concerned with leadership. In most small groups faced with a task, two kinds of leaders emerge. The first kind of leader is devoted to fulfilling the task of the group efficiently. He is usually not the person in the group who is liked best by the others, but the members concede that he is the one with the best ideas for getting the job done. For example, a group has to solve a mathematics problem, the best mathematician in the group may become the task leader. Sociologist Robert Bales has called the first kind of leader an *instrumental leader* because he functions to spur the group to accomplish its task.

The second kind of leader is devoted to keeping the morale in the group at a high level and to making sure that the relations among members are friendly. He is usually the person who is best liked in the group. For example, if the group has trouble solving the math problem, a member with a good sense of humor may break the tension. Bales has called the second kind of leader an *affective leader*, because he functions to keep the emotional tone of the group at a high level.

TWO TYPES OF LEADERS

It is unusual for the same person to perform the roles of instrumental and affective leader. These two roles seem to involve clashing requirements. The good instrumental leader attempts to make the group into an efficient machine for accomplishing the task. He tends to ignore individual differences and would prefer not to recognize unique needs. The instrumental leader judges people according to their performance and tends not to care about personal qualities. The instrumental leader tends to take the role of others in social positions more than he takes the role of particular others. He sees people as means to an end. In the group solving the math problem the instrumental leader would judge everyone according to the standards of ability in math and effort expended on the problem.

The good affective leader attempts to make the group into a harmonious gathering of colleagues. He stresses individual differences, has a sense of humor, and cares a great deal about personal qualities. The affective leader tends to take the role of particular others more than he takes the role of others in social positions. He sees people primarily as ends in themselves. In the group solving the math problem the affective leader would try to make sure that nobody became too tense, frustrated, and angry.

While there is a tension between the roles of instrumental leader and affective leader, both roles are necessary to successful cooperation. Left to himself, the purely instrumental leader will treat people as cogs in a machine, and will eventually bring about a rebellion against himself. Left to himself, the purely affective leader will stress good fellowship so much that members will completely lose sight of the task at hand. Instrumental and affective leaders complement one another and seem to appear wherever human beings cooperate. An example of this balance is in the Western cultural ideal of the family, in which the father is the instrumental leader and the mother is the affective leader.

Other studies of small groups have centered on the kinds of authority that leaders exercise. In a famous experiment, Lewin, Lippitt, and White compared three groups of children making masks. In one group the adult leader was an autocrat, giving the children orders without consulting them. In the second group the adult leader left the children to do as they pleased within very broad limits. In the third group the adult leader helped the children decide by majority vote the way that they wanted to make the masks. In each case, the leader left the room in which the children were working and social scientists observed the behavior of the three groups. In the first group, where authority was autocratic, the children could hardly cooperate at all. No work was done and each child blamed the others when mistakes were made. The second group, in which the children were relatively left to do as they pleased, fared better in output than the group where authority was autocratic. However, there was still very little cooperation. The third group, in which the children helped decide what they would do by democratic methods, had the highest output and greatest cooperation when the leader left. This kind of experiment has been repeated in various contexts, usually with the same results. This has led many social psychologists to state that cooperation in seeking a goal is more likely when political processes are democratic than when they are dictatorial or absent. In practical application this has meant that workers are often "consulted" about their jobs, even though they have ultimately very little to say about their working conditions. However, when one's participation will have a genuine effect, it is likely that democracy will increase cooperation.

COMPETITION

Competition is the human relation in which people attempt to gain maximum shares of a scarce good. As in the case of cooperation, there are two major kinds of competition. In its central meaning, competition involves two or more people, aware of one another and aware of their opposition. This kind of competition is illustrated by two children competing for the time and affection of their mother. They both want their mother's attention and both are filled with resentment when the other gains it. They will use a wide variety of strategies and tactics to attain their goals, including attempting to outdo one another at being good, pleading illness or having accidents to attract attention, tattling on their rival, or even being bad just so the mother will spend time with them. This kind of competition can be quite vicious, but it remains competition and not conflict as long as the opponents both seek the mother's time and attention rather than one another's ruin. In modern societies a second type of competition becomes important. Here, one competes in complex role systems against people he may not even know for scarce goods such as money, social position, and influence. This kind of impersonal competition is illustrated by high school seniors throughout the United States competing for limited places in junior colleges, colleges, and universities. They attempt to make high scores on nationwide college entrance examinations, but have no control over the actions of the vast majority of their opponents and no control over the quality of education they received in high school. Both impersonal cooperation and impersonal competition are important parts of contemporary American life.

Americans often use the image of a game to describe many aspects of their social existence. *Games* are controlled social situations in which competition is the dominant human relation. They are sets of rules defining a contest, the meaning of victory, and the rights and duties of the opponents. Thus, games are primarily sets of roles. For example, baseball is a contest between two teams, in which each side attempts to score the maximum number of runs while holding the other side to a minimum number of runs. The different positions filled by members of the opposing teams are defined by roles. Thus, the batter has a right to go to first base if he is hit by a pitched ball, but has the duty to try to avoid being hit. If the batter intentionally puts himself in front of a pitched ball he will be declared "out" by the umpire, who has the role of enforcing the rules. In most games the cultural definition of role as a set of known rights and duties is nearly the same as the social definition of role as expected behavior. It is relatively easy to take the role of the other, and predictions of behavior in situations defined by the rules are likely to be highly accurate. There is usually no cultural conflict, involving competing role definitions, and opponents normally share the same goal (winning), recognize the legitimacy of the rules and accept the authority of the umpire, when one is present. Disagreements take place over applications of the rules to particular situations (was a pitch a ball or a strike) rather than over the rules themselves or the goal of victory. In games where groups or teams compete, cooperation within each team underlies competition between the teams.

The fact that all participants in games generally agree upon the goal, rules, and procedures for applying the rules makes game behavior highly predictable. People will tend to strive toward the goal while keeping within the rules. Stability is favored even more by the fact that the rules stay the same throughout the game. The controlled and predictable nature of games leads some Americans to wish that life were a game or even to believe that it is one. Phrases like "the game of politics," "the game of marriage" and "the game of love" betray a wish that human existence were simpler. Another feature of games is that they only involve a part of the self and ultimately are not decisive in human existence. Thus, people who cannot face human tragedy will often treat their social relations as competitive games. In related cases, people who are social failures and do not want to face the fact that either an unjust social order or their own inadequacies have caused their ruin will shrug their shoulders and say, "That was the breaks of the game." People who consciously take human existence seriously will often become upset when others "play games" with them. Americans are more likely to use the image of game to describe their social existence than other peoples because of their belief, stemming from early Puritan social compacts and the United States Constitution, that social institutions are consciously planned by human beings who then agree to abide by the rules that they have set up. When these rules involve competition, social institutions do have some resemblance to games.

The fact that games are controlled social situations in which competition is the dominant social relation and that they are important in American life has led social scientists to use games in an experimental setting as a way of understanding competitive relations. Some experiments have contrasted the relations of competition and cooperation. These experiments make a bridge between the studies of groups performing tasks and groups and individuals competing with one another. In one study people were told to play a game in which the object was to get a cone out of a bottle with a piece of string. The

IS LIFE A GAME?

GAME — LIFE

EVERYONE KNOWS THE RULES — THE RULES ARE NOT CLEAR

EVERYONE ACCEPTS THE RULES — DIFFERENT PEOPLE PLAY BY DIFFERENT RULES

EVERYONE OBEYS THE RULES — RULES ARE MADE TO BE BROKEN

THE RULES STAY THE SAME DURING THE GAME — THE RULES KEEP CHANGING

THE RULES AFFECT EVERYONE IN THE SAME WAY — THERE IS DISCRIMINATION

THE OUTCOME IS NOT A MATTER OF LIFE OR DEATH — THE OUTCOME OF LIFE IS DEATH

CAN YOU REALLY SAY THAT LIFE IS A GAME?

people were divided into two groups. In one group the subjects were told that they would be rewarded for successful cooperation in performing the task. In the other group the subjects were told that they would be given rewards and assessed fines depending upon their individual success. Social psychologist W. J. H. Sprott points out that "not surprisingly there were endless traffic jams" in the competitive group, while the cooperators "proceeded with elegant coordination."[2] He adds, however, that this kind of experiment does not demonstrate that cooperation is invariably a more productive social relation than competition: "A group of people competing *separately*, so that their actions do not interfere with one another, may be more efficient in total output than if competition was ruled out."[3] Generally, however, social psychologists have found that when people in task groups are given more reasons to compete than to cooperate, success in accomplishing the tasks decreases. People attempt to show that their contributions are more important than those of others and refuse to listen closely to what others are saying.

Instead of comparing the relations of cooperation and competition, some research has concentrated on the internal dynamics of competition. A group of social scientists has extensively analyzed the strategies that people use to win when they play games. These social scientists, or game theorists, have described a large number of games mathematically and have figured out the most efficient strategies for players. For example, some game theorists believe that competition between political parties is like a game in which the players try to get the most benefits possible. They say that parties with a large majority will tend to get rid of some of their supporters so that there will be less people with whom to share the benefits of victory. Parties in the minority will attempt to appeal to these outcasts. Political scientist William Riker, who has presented this view, claims that the search for a "minimum winning coalition" is partly responsible for political change.[4] The majority party may cut back too far, and the minority may be successful in winning members to its side. In Riker's model of competition, the fence-sitter is the person who gains the most when competition is intense.

Conclusions like those of Riker have been disputed by Theodore Caplow. In the games that Caplow set up, participants were not treated as equals, but were assigned different weights of importance. In a three-person game, with coalitions permitted, one person was assigned a weight of four, another a weight of three, and the last a weight of two. Once people learned the game, they realized that any combination of two people would defeat the other person. However, coalitions tended to be made up mostly by those with the weights of three and two. Those with weights of four tended to demand larger shares of the spoils than a rational calculation of benefit would have given them. This finding led Caplow to conclude that factors of power and status, as well as economic calculation, affect the relation of competition. It is important to note that Caplow's experiments do not necessarily show that Riker's arguments are incorrect. In Riker's experiments, people were given equal weight, so considerations of power and status did not intrude. Of course, in everyday life power and status are closely bound up with economic activity.[5]

The study of experimental gaming points up certain aspects of the competitive relation while deemphasizing others. In games, one is conscious that he faces an opponent, and both sides are eager to gain advantage. There is no doubt that many Americans interpret a large number of their relations this way. They see "labor" pitted against "management" with government as the "umpire." They see husbands and wives engaged in a "battle of the sexes." They tend to lose sight of the fact that competition in ordinary life is only partly like competition in games. Frequently in ordinary life, the rules are not very well defined, there is no impartial and accepted umpire, the rules change in the middle of the competition, and emotions get in the way of calculation. Further, the rules are often biased in favor of certain groups. For example, if only those with a degree can get certain jobs, those deprived of educational opportunities will not be equal contestants in the "game of life." Most important, the research into competition fails to consider the important distinction between striving to attain a standard of excellence and striving to get the most of a scarce good, or to win.

WHERE DO YOU FIT ?

In ordinary life much of what passes for competition is the attempt to achieve. Achievement motivation and competition get mixed up when the fruits of achievement are used as standards for distributing rewards such as promotions, raises, and prizes. The person who achieved excellence was not necessarily motivated by the hope of winning a prize. He may have simply wanted to do his job well. For example, the winner of a talent contest could have been interested in turning in a good performance rather than in winning the prize money. However, when rewards are distributed on the basis of achievement it is well to remember that whether or not the person intends to compete for a scarce good, he is engaged in impersonal competition at the very least. The reason to keep achievement motivation separate from competition is that the difference between intrinsic and extrinsic rewards is maintained. Many people believe that if such practices as keeping steep salary differences and strict grading systems were eliminated, human progress would cease. They believe that human beings perform well only when there is a carrot in front of them and a stick behind them. However, there are intrinsic rewards in doing an interesting and challenging job well, and extrinsic rewards in the praise and appreciation of colleagues. If work becomes more interesting and challenging, it may be possible for competition to give way somewhat to achievement motivation.

CONFLICT

The line between competition and conflict is quite hazy. Conflict is the human relation in which people attempt to defeat each other's purposes for the sake of hurting the others. Thus, the same outward actions may be involved in relations of competition and conflict. A businessman may lie about the character of a competitor so that he can increase his business (competition), or he may tell the same lie just to damage his opponent (conflict).

One of the findings of social psychologists who have studied competitive relations in small groups is that under certain conditions, competition very easily becomes conflict. In games where people bargain with one another to make up coalitions, they can sometimes break promises. Frequently, when promises are broken, even in an experimental setting, the injured party will vow to make the other person "pay" for his betrayal. This will sometimes lead to the injured party's hurting his own chances of winning the game just so he can make the other person suffer. When a person gives up his opportunity to achieve a goal that he desires merely to hurt another person, there is a clear case of the shift from competition to conflict. Many factors can cause the shift from competition to conflict, or from cooperation or concord to conflict. Betrayal is a very important cause of conflict, as is the idea that another person has broken the rules of "fair" competition. Conflict is also brought about by the judgment that a person or group has been treated unjustly. When people believe both that they deserve certain rights and that they are prevented from exercising them by a particular group of people, they are likely to engage in conflict with those whom they see in their way.

Like cooperation and competition, conflict can be personal or impersonal In personal conflict people attempt to hurt one another on an individual basis. They recognize one another as human beings, each with the ability to plan and appreciate, but they try to thwart each other's plans and to deprive one another of enjoyment.

Impersonal conflict is basically what was called cultural conflict in Chapter Two. Here people try to prevent others from living up to their various role definitions, or try to force new role definitions upon others. Thus, personal conflict is bound up with the individual and creative "I," while impersonal conflict is connected closely with the social "me." A good example of a personal conflict is a fist fight over an insult. The opponents both agree on the role definition of a man. If a man is insulted he is supposed to be prepared to defend his honor through violence if the other does not take back the insult. In this case, there is almost a pure personal conflict. The person who provokes it wants to hurt another person, while the insulted person soon forgets that he is fighting to defend his honor and turns his full attention to making his opponent suffer. This conflict, and many others like it, definitely do not involve clashing role definitions.

In the case of impersonal conflict, clashing role definitions are at stake. For example, in religious violence, such as that between Catholics and Protestants in northern Ireland, the opponents are attempting to injure people who accept certain role definitions. They do not attack people as individuals, but as members or representatives of a religious faith.

CONCORD

The relation opposite to conflict is concord. Concord is the human relation in which people attempt to aid one another in realizing their goals. The most elementary form of concord is *reciprocity* or *exchange*, in which people give aid in exchange for aid. Sociologists such as George Homans and Peter Blau believe that exchange is the most basic social relation. They view exchange as a relation in which people make an investment to gain a reward. One will help a co-worker by giving him advice about how to solve a problem on the job with the expectation that he will be given help when it is needed in the future. Exchanges cause mutual expectations and are the basis of many roles.

Difficulty arises when the person who receives aid cannot adequately return the favor in kind. This is not a significant problem in small groups characterized by a culture with few tools and relatively unspecialized symbols. On the frontier a person who received aid when he built his barn would help his neighbors put up their barns. However, in the contemporary world, where tools are complex, symbols specialized, and abilities possessed unequally, many exchanges appear to be unequal. How can the person who is aided by a skilled colleague balance the scales? Blau points out that in contemporary society he is unlikely to give him material repayment. However, he can give him both prestige and power. He can tell others about the skill and competence of his helper and can praise him. He can also allow his helper to make certain decisions for him, giving him power. Exchange can lead to severe conflict when expectations that have been built up are not honored.

Not all relations of concord are used up by exchange and repayment in kind. Beyond exchange is altruism, in which a person gives aid to another without any expectation of reward. Like the other relations, altruism can be personal or impersonal. In its personal form altruism involves one person aiding another in realizing a goal within a primary group relation. In its impersonal form altruism involves one person aiding another whom he does not know. While personal altruism remains important in the contemporary world in such contexts as friendship and the family, impersonal altruism has gained in significance with the growing complexity, scale, and specialization of modern culture. Organized charity, through such agencies as religious organizations, governments, humanitarian organizations, community agencies, and businesses, plays an important part in American life. Often such organized charity fails to reflect altruism, as when people are pressured to "give" at work, or when high pressure appeals are made to their guilt. In such cases charity becomes more like exchange than like altruism. One gives to keep the respect of his colleagues, or because of the good feeling that he gets when he believes that he is free of guilt.

The existence of instances in which exchange hides behind the cloak of altruism should not lead to the conclusion that altruism does not appear in human existence. It is not always possible to prove that an act was selfish (in the sense that it was not directed primarily to help another) unless one resorts to hidden motives of which nobody in the relation was aware. It is probably true that the maintenance of human existence depends upon some altruism. If people never over-fulfilled their roles or created new ones it is unlikely that morale would be high enough to sustain social life. (This, at least, was the belief of Auguste Comte, one of the founders of modern sociology.)

THE HOUSE THAT JACK BUILT (RE-REVISITED)

1. JACK JUST PUT IN A FLOWER GARDEN

2. HIS FRIEND TONY HELPED HIM PLANT IT
   (PERSONAL COOPERATION)

3. THE SEEDS WERE DEVELOPED IN A RESEARCH
   LABORATORY (IMPERSONAL COOPERATION)

4. HE WANTS THE BEST LOOKING GARDEN ON THE BLOCK
   (PERSONAL COMPETITION)

5. HE WANTS THE GARDEN MAGAZINE "BEST GARDEN OF THE
   YEAR AWARD" (IMPERSONAL COMPETITION)

6. HE PUNCHED HIS NEIGHBOR IN THE NOSE AFTER THE
   NEIGHBOR WALKED ON HIS FLOWER BED (PERSONAL
   CONFLICT)

7. HIS NEIGHBOR WALKED ON THE FLOWER BED BECAUSE
   JACK IS A MEMBER OF THE SOCIETY FOR SNAKE
   WORSHIP (IMPERSONAL CONFLICT)

8. HE PAID A LOCAL MERCHANT FOR FERTILIZER
   (EXCHANGE)

9. HE SENDS FLOWERS TO PATIENTS AT THE LOCAL
   HOSPITAL (ALTRUISM)

SUMMARY

Human relations arise from the basic fact that human beings stimulate one another through their actions. Underlying the basic types of human relation is the relation of association. When mere association is engaged in as an end in itself, sociability appears. Sociability is the sheer pleasure of being among others, and is observable evidence that human beings are not solitary creatures.

There are four basic types of human relation. In cooperation human beings help one another to reach a common goal. In personal cooperation, people all want to achieve the same result. An example is a group of people pushing a car to get it started. In impersonal cooperation, people aid one another because they receive extrinsic rewards for doing so. An example is a factory worker on an assembly line who works because he is getting wages.

In competition people vie with one another for scarce resources. In personal competition they are aware of one another, as in the case of two children competing for their mother's attention. In impersonal competition people may not even be aware that they are competing, as in the nationwide competition for college entrance.

In conflict, people attempt to prevent one another from achieving goals. Personal conflict pits human beings against one another as individuals, while cultural conflict opposes people who are representatives of clashing role definitions.

In concord, people attempt to aid one another in reaching fulfillment. In exchange one person aids another with the expectation of help in return, while in altruism one aids another without the expectation of reciprocity or repayment. While altruism is perhaps not as common as the other relations, its occurrence is probably necessary to the continuation of social existence.

The wide variety of relations leads to the question of whether anything can be said about people in general. The ways in which people organize their roles and control their relations is the subject of the next chapter.

Notes

[1] Don Martindale, *The Nature and Types of Sociological Theory* (Boston: Houghton Mifflin Company, 1960), p. 241.

[2] W. J. H. Sprott, *Human Groups*, (Baltimore: Penguin Books, Inc., 1967), pp. 117-118.

[3] Sprott, *Human Groups*, p. 118.

[4] William H. Riker, *The Theory of Political Coalitions* (New Haven: Yale University Press, 1962).

[5] R. P. Cuzzort, *Humanity and Modern Sociological Thought* (New York: Holt, Rinehart and Winston, Inc., 1969).

Suggested Readings

Berne, E. *The Games People Play*, New York: Grove Press, Inc., 1964 (paper).

Fanon, F. *The Wretched of the Earth*, New York: Grove Press, Inc., 1968 (paper).

Morris, D. *The Naked Ape: A Zoologist's Study of the Human Animal*, New York: McGraw-Hill Book Company, Inc., 1967.

Olmstead, M. S. *The Small Group*, New York: Random House, Inc. 1959 (paper).

Sherif, M. *Psychology of Social Norms*, New York: Harper & Row, Publishers, 1965 (paper).

Sprott, W. H. *Human Groups*, Baltimore: Penguin Books, Inc., 1958 (paper).

Storr, A. *Human Aggression*, New York: Atheneum Publishers, 1968.

Whyte, W. F. *Street Corner Society*, Chicago: The University of Chicago Press, 1955 (paper).

CHAPTER TEN: ROLE INTEGRATION

Thus far, four major problems have been discussed in this book. First, there was an explanation of the way in which human beings become participants in cultural systems, actors in social processes, and partners or opponents in human relations. Here, the process of socialization was at the center of attention. The development of the human being from an infant expressing demands, to a child capable of taking the role of particular others, to a mature person able to take the roles of others in social positions was described. This description involved a difference between two parts of the self, the "me" and the "I." The "me," or social self, is made up of the various roles that the person has learned to take, and to which he refers as guides when he decides how to act in various situations. The "I," or individual and creative self, makes plans for the future and sometimes goes beyond the role definitions that the person has learned. Social thought in the twentieth century has been a dialogue between the "me" and the "I."

The second problem discussed related to culture. Culture was defined as the learned heritage of human beings. Here, some of the aspects of the social self were examined. Role was defined as a set of rights and duties used in the performance of a task. In their cultural sense, roles are learned by human beings, and can be accepted or rejected by them in thought and action. In any complicated culture there are many competing definitions of role to fit many tasks. Some people believe that the teacher should be a resource person, while others believe that he should be a judge.

The third problem discussed followed from the second. Here, the processes of putting culture into action were described. Role was defined as a set of expected behaviors in the performance of a task, such as the behaviors expected of a factory worker on the job. This definition resulted from the fact that in concrete, or specific, situations in social life people combine their abilities to take the roles of others in social positions and to take the roles of particular others. For example, the teacher may find out that in a particular school he is expected to be a stern judge. Four major social processes and four key groups of roles relating to them were defined by looking at the ways in which people can use culture. Economic roles stem from the fact that human beings create, preserve, destroy, and distribute culture. For example, they build, sell, and buy houses. Political roles stem from the fact that people coordinate the various uses of culture. For example, zoning laws determine what kind of houses can be built in a certain area. Educational roles are related to the fact that human beings pass on information to one another about culture. For example, houses are built after blueprints are consulted. Appreciative roles are related to the fact that people enjoy and consume culture. People live in houses with their families. Economic roles are aimed at the portion of culture known as tools, political roles are aimed at rules, educational roles are aimed at symbols, and appreciative roles are aimed at products. All four social processes are necessary for human existence and together they define human action.

The fourth problem discussed in this book centered on the dynamics or driving forces, or human relations. Within the four major social processes are relations defining how people act together to put culture into action. When they are concerned with objects of culture, people can cooperate or compete. In cooperation people aid one another in reaching a goal. In competition people oppose one another for shares of scarce goods. When they are concerned with one another's plans, people can engage in conflict or concord. In

THE SELF AND OTHERS

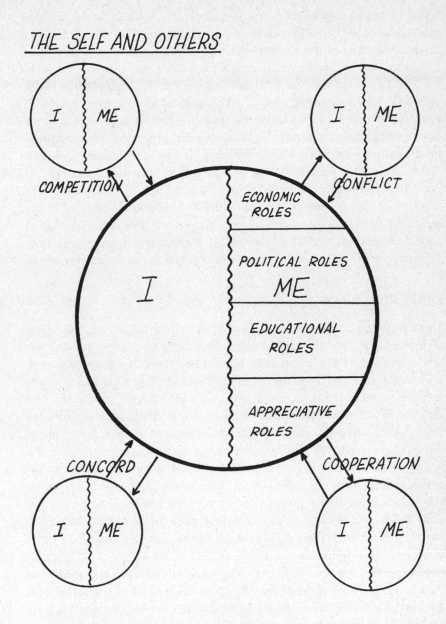

conflict human beings try to defeat one another. In concord they try to help one another. Role definitions often include directions about where and when cooperation, competition, conflict, and concord are suitable.

The previous discussions make a circle and come to a climax in the problem of how the various roles that make up the social self are combined with one another into a meaningful whole. The study of social science begins with how the human animal becomes the human being. It ends with how the human being organizes patterns of culture, social processes, and human relations into an order that has some meaning for him. This organizing process within the human personality has two parts. The first part deals with the relation of roles to one another within the social self, or "me." This is the problem of *role integration*. The second part concerns the relation of the social self to the individual and creative self, or "I." This is the problem of *true existence and freedom* in a world of bureaucratic organizations. Both problems are of great importance to human beings in our present-day world.

DIFFERENCES OF ROLES

Throughout the discussion it was assumed that the social self was a definable unit with some structure and that the roles making up the "me" fit together into a pattern. Is this assumption reasonable? There is much evidence to support the view that the social self in the contemporary world does *not* have a definite structure. Looking back over the topics covered, one sees a great diversity in kinds of roles. First, from the cultural viewpoint, there are competing definitions of the same role present in current social life. For example, some people claim that the role of a clergyman should be to convince his congregation to support movements for political change and to set an example of decision-making social action. Other people say that the clergyman's role should be to aid the members of his congregation in meeting their personal problems and tragedies, and to convert more people to the faith. In this conflict, the competing role definitions are opposed on many issues.

Second, even within the same role definition there may be differing requirements. For example, even if a clergyman has decided to play the role of a person encouraging social change, he may still have problems deciding what kinds of political action are fitting. If he is within the Judaeo-Christian tradition he has an obligation to avoid violence. However, militant political action frequently brings on violence. How can he solve the conflict between the duties to further social change and to avoid violence? Both duties are within the same role definition, and they sometimes may conflict.

Third, every person performs more than one role, and the definitions of different roles may conflict with one another. For example, some parents who find their children taking drugs are faced with a serious conflict. The role of good citizen includes the duty to report violations of law to the police authorities. However, the role of good parent includes the duty to protect children from suffering and unhappiness. On the cultural level there are role conflicts between competing definitions of the same role, competing requirements of the same role definition, and competing requirements of more than one role. These conflicts occur when a person believes that he cannot do one or more of his duties without failing to do one or more of his other duties.

Other serious role conflicts occur because of tensions between cultural and social definitions of role. A person may have chosen one out of a number of competing role definitions as valid, smoothed over the conflicts within that role, and reconciled that role with other roles, and still be faced with problems. He may find that expected behaviors clash with formal rights and duties. For example, a young engineer may feel obligated to design products that will last and be easy to service. Yet he may find out that the corporation that has hired him expects him to design products that will wear out after several years of use and will be so difficult to fix that they must be thrown away when they break down. A soldier may feel obligated to avoid injuring civilians and yet find out that his officers and fellow soldiers expect him to take part in needless slaughter. Further, the same kinds of role conflicts that occur among cultural definitions may occur between social expectations. Different particular others may have clashing expectations. If the captain expects one to avoid injuring civilians and the lieutenant expects one to kill them, who should be satisfied? This kind of problem is like the one of choosing among competing role definitions. Also, within any set of expectations there may be conflicts. What is one to do if the captain wants a village leveled and nobody within it hurt? Finally, expectations regarding different roles can conflict. A wife may expect her husband to come home early from a night with the boys, while the boys may expect their friend to stay out late.

Yet other serious role conflicts are related to requirements that one take part in clashing social relations. At church a person may be told that he should seek peace in all his relations, while in his labor union he may learn that he is supposed to do his part for victory in a bitter conflict with management. A businessman may be told by his superiors both that he should cooperate with his co-workers and that he will be promoted on the basis of how much better than his co-workers he performs. Tensions among requirements to take part in clashing human relations provoke some of the most serious role conflicts in Western civilization. Here, the broadest boundaries of a person's life may be involved in the decision.

Should one adopt the role of human being that defines life as a jungle in which only the fittest survives after difficult competition and vicious conflict with his fellows? Should one adopt the role of human being that defines life as capable of love and requires the individual to make an effort to put love into the world? Should one adopt the role of human being that defines life as divided between love and peace within one's own cultural group and hatred and war when cultural groups meet with one another? Should one adopt the role of human being that requires the individual to take part in whatever relations are suggested in the various social processes, whether or not they clash? Role conflicts related to human relations often present people with their most severe moral problems.

All of the various role conflicts meet in the social self. It is the social self that carries the cultural definitions of role that the person has learned. The individual self asks, "What would a teacher do if I did this?" The social self answers as best it can. It is the social self that carries the social definitions of role used by the person in daily activities. The individual self asks, "What would my social science teacher do if I did this?" The social self answers as best it can. It is the social self that carries the definitions of social situations and relations. The individual self asks whether it is proper or expected to take part in cooperation, competition, conflict, or concord, and the social self answers as best it can. The answers of the social self depend upon the success in which the various roles of the individual have been *integrated*, or made into a meaningful pattern. Are the conflicts of role resolved by the individual? If they are, how does role integration take place? These are among the most important general questions that people in the twentieth century attempt to answer.

RESOLVING ROLE CONFLICT

If the social self was merely a dumping ground for all of the role definitions present in a person's cultural and social environment, people would not display any lasting structure in their actions. From one moment to the next behavior would vary. The stable, or unvarying, expectations necessary to carrying out social life would disappear and the situation would be just as confused as it would be in the absence of roles. However, people do display order in their actions, and this can be shown by several factors. First, in complex cultures people do not know all of the role definitions present in the culture. They may not even be aware of the competing definitions of the roles that they do perform. They may not consider different definitions as serious options. This means that each individual is aware of only a part of the culture. The roles defining this portion may not be in serious conflict and, therefore, the person will not experience severe role conflict. For example, the clergyman may not be aware that some people say that he should be a social activist.

Second, for reasons that have nothing to do with the roles themselves, some role definitions are more appealing than others. The enforcement of role obligations makes up the system of social control. If people are rewarded with desired products for performing certain roles and are not given such products for performing other roles, they will tend to behave in the ways that are rewarded. For example, a soldier may be rewarded with extra leave for performing unpleasant tasks. It is important to remember that people will not always seek material gains. Political radicals, religious martyrs, and intellectuals have sometimes sacrificed products for principle. Further, twentieth-century history has shown many times that cultural minorities cannot be bought off easily by more powerful cultural groups. Role obligations are also enforced by violence. If people are physically punished for performing some roles and for failing to perform others, they will tend to behave in ways that do not bring on physical punishment. A soldier may be put in the stockade if he does not follow orders. Again, this statement describes a tendency, not an iron law of behavior. Faced with severe violence, cultural minorities and economically deprived groups around the world continue to make their claims with militance.

Finally, role obligations are enforced by praise and blame. People will tend to do what will bring them praise and to avoid doing what will bring them blame. A soldier may be given a medal for heroism. This statement also describes a tendency rather than an iron law. People give up the praise of some and seek the praise of others. They sometimes reject praise when desire for products, fear of violence, or commitment to principle is involved in a situation. Thus, while the workings of social control are important in accounting for the fact that most people do not behave in a random and chaotic manner, a large proportion of cases of role conflict remain unexplained by these mechanisms.

People go beyond the processes of social control in two important ways. First, they seek consistency or the absence of change, among their various role obligations. Second, they make plans, sometimes creating new roles in the process, which bring their role obligations into a meaningful order. The rest of this chapter will describe the search for consistency, while the last chapter will describe the creative "I" as it meets the major problems of contemporary life.

In discussing the ways in which people attempt to make their various role obligations consistent it is necessary to remember several important differences. First, one must see the difference between obligations which are logically contradictory and those which clash psychologically. When duties are logically contradictory, it means that they violate the law of noncontradiction. The *law of noncontradiction* states that an idea and its negation cannot both be true at the same time, that "A" and "not-A" cannot both be true. For example, if I tell a person that I expect him to kill a certain individual and also to save that individual's life, I am telling him to behave in a contradictory manner. He cannot meet my expectations. While conflicts within roles usually are not logically contradictory, logical contradiction does exist between different roles. For example, there is logical contradiction between the Judaeo-Christian commandment to love one's neighbor and the commands to hate issued by certain interest groups.

Logically contradictory obligations present some of the most difficult cases of role conflict, because there can be no compromise or meeting between them. Most role conflicts, however, involve *psychological contradiction*. Here, the person feels that doing one duty correctly keeps him from fully doing another duty. For example, there is nothing logically contradictory about a clergyman working for social change and attempting to avoid violence. Such a person could encourage and take part in movements of nonviolent resistance to social injustice. However, the socially conscious and active clergyman could still feel a psychological conflict among the obligations. He might wonder whether or not nonviolence can be a successful plan for change in the present-day world. Does his nonviolence interfere with his commitment to gain social justice? He might wonder whether or not his activities in search of social change will bring on violence from the authorities or cause violence in those within the social movement who are impatient. Does his commitment to gain social justice interfere with his quest for nonviolence? This kind of psychological contradiction is the most common kind of role conflict. Very rarely are role obligations bluntly, logically contradictory. Rather, people experience a tension among their various obligations and worry that they may be logically contradictory in the end.

A second important distinction is between incompatible, or disagreeing, obligations and contradictory obligations. When obligations are incompatible, they actually cannot both be fulfilled. A man cannot fulfill the obligations of driving within the speed limit and driving a relative to the hospital as fast as possible. However, as he is driving to the hospital he may experience no contradiction between the two obligations, because he forgets about the speed limit or believes that obeying it is unimportant. Thus, the actual fact of role conflict (incompatibility) must be distinguished from the experience of role conflict (contradiction). It is possible for a person to be committed deeply to incompatible obligations and to fail to recognize the conflict. For example, many people who fail to do school assignments and flunk courses are committed to academic success, but are also committed to being independent of authority. They may not recognize that their dislike of authority is behind their failure to study. However, psychologists have found that when this happens, the person is likely to experience suffering that he cannot account for, or behaviors that interfere with reaching his stated goals. While it is quite important to keep separate incompatibility and experienced contradiction, they are related to one another. People can feel that there is a contradiction between two obligations when, in fact, they are quite compatible, or agreeable. A soldier may feel a contradiction between the obligation to defeat the enemy and the obligation not to murder civilians, when these obligations are actually compatible. People can also be unaware that two obligations are, in fact, incompatible. A politician may not be aware that making false promises is actually incompatible with maintaining unity of the group. In most cases, however, there is at least a minimum experience of contradiction when important duties are incompatible.

COPING MECHANISMS

There are three major ways in which the person can deal with role conflicts. First, he can pretend that the conflicts do not exist. For example, a person who believes that he should "turn the other cheek" when faced with hatred may demand the death penalty for convicted murderers. He may not be aware of the conflict between the two principles or he may claim that there is no conflict at all.

Second, a person can try to make a compromise between the conflicting obligations. For example, a man may be faced with a conflict between the obligations involved in being a "good" father and the duties involved in practicing his profession. A doctor may be expected to be "on call" for his patients 24 hours a day, while a father may be expected to devote long periods of undivided attention to his children. The person faced with this kind of conflict may compromise by setting certain days aside for his family while giving his work top priority the rest of the time.

Third, a person may choose one of the conflicting obligations as more important than the others. For example, the doctor may reject the role of "good" father and give his work top priority at all times. A fourth way of resolving role conflicts, creating a new role definition, is far less frequent than the other three and is far more difficult for the person attempting it.

DENIAL OF CONFLICT

The most widespread way of coping with role conflict is to pretend that it does not exist, or to convince oneself that it does not exist. There are several ways in which this is done. First, the person may *compartmentalize* his roles. In modern societies, marked by a high degree of space and time specialization and separation of human activities, it is possible for someone to be one person at certain places and times and another person at other places and times. The divided self is a trait of twentieth-century life. The division of the self is made possible by the separation in space and time of such major processes as creating, preserving, destroying, and distributing culture, coordinating the uses of culture, transmitting information about culture, and appreciating culture. The most striking example of the divided self in modern life is the businessman-civic leader-family man-pillar of the church. This compound social self, though no longer a symbol of American life since the Great Depression, still keeps a certain importance. As a businessman this person plays the role of economic man, attempting to maximize profits and to gain as many advantages for his firm as possible. He will not spend any more money than he has to on controlling environmental pollution, will attempt to have tax breaks for his industry written into the law, and will try to maximize his rights and minimize his duties in relations with consumers. He justifies this behavior on the grounds that in a free enterprise system it is his obligation as a businessman to maximize profits for the stockholders. The stockholders have invested money in the firm so that they can gain a higher return than they would elsewhere, not so that they can finance social improvements out of their own pockets. If pollution is to be eliminated, all competitors must make the same sacrifice. No corporation, claims the businessman, should go out of its way to cut its profit. If a firm is more public spirited than the rest it will have to raise prices, take a cut in sales, and eventually go out of business; or it will have to keep prices the same, take a reduction in profit, and eventually lose investment capital.

As a civic leader this person plays the role of protector of the public interest. He is deeply involved with work for community charities and service clubs. He tries to get businessmen to donate money, facilities, and products to charitable and philanthropic drives. He claims that it is the civic duty of businessmen and others who have benefited from the community to give their share for supporting hospitals, cultural events, and social-service agencies such as half-way houses for alcoholics, adoption centers, youth groups, and medical-research foundations. He argues that those who do not contribute what he believes to be their "fair shares" are selfish and fail to take the public interest into account. He no longer plays the role of economic man, but instead plays the role of philanthropic servant who sacrifices time and money for the betterment of the community.

As a family man this person stresses concord and cooperation in his relations rather than competition. While at work he is quick to demand that "lazy" workers be fired and in the community he urges strict measures against rebellious youth, drug abusers, and speeders. At home he permits the weaknesses of his children and tends to excuse their flaws as "part of growing up." At work and in the community he may even go so far as to claim that a "permissive" society is destroying the morality of the nation. He may justify laying off workers or cutting off their overtime as necessary measures to trim the "fat" from the economy and to encourage a more serious and hard-working labor force. He may justify stiff fines and prison sentences for minor offenders so that they will learn that "crime does not pay." However, he may try to make sure that his son gets an interesting summer job with the firm that leaves him plenty of time off for recreation and the freedom necessary in "growing up." If his son gets a traffic ticket or is arrested for a drug violation, he may attempt to "stand behind him all the way," get him the best lawyer possible, and bend every effort to prevent a "blot" appearing on his record. He will justify this behavior on the principle that a father's duty is to protect his family in good times and bad, and will argue, "If I do not help my son, who will?" Here, he plays the role neither of economic man nor of community leader, but instead plays the role of protector of home and hearth.

As a pillar of the church, this person stresses the need for love and justice in the world and claims that forgiveness heals the wounds caused by conflict. He argues that one should not give his soul to material wealth and strongly regrets the behavior of economic man who is always interested in maximizing his advantage. He believes that love is a far more powerful force than revenge and punishment, and that people adopt violence too easily as a means of solving their problems. He believes that the law of love applies to all human beings, not just to one's family, and that it is better to give than to receive.

He feels renewed after church services on Sunday and gains new hope that the world may someday be a better place to live. He does not believe that he must justify his behavior because its goodness is self-evident and it follows from the will of God. Here, the person is playing the role neither of economic man, civic leader, nor of protector of hearth and home, but instead is playing the role of good Christian.

THE FOUR FACES OF NOWHERE MAN (COMPARTMENTALIZATION)

The businessman, civic leader, family man, and pillar of the church compartmentalizes his various roles. He does not notice that there is a conflict between the principle of service that he applies in the community and the principle of profit that he applies in business. Neither does he notice that his permissiveness with his children conflicts with the ideal that he upholds of a nonpermissive society. He also does not notice that the principle of Christian love conflicts with the principle that the businessman should maximize his rights and minimize his duties with respect to the consumer. All of these conflicts, and many others, are resolved simply because different roles are played at different places and times, and in different situations. Religious considerations are not suitable in the board room on weekdays, and business considerations are not suitable in church on Sundays. Family problems are forgotten at civic luncheons in the daytime, and charity drives and civic boosterism are forgotten in the evening at the dinner table.

In discussing the workings of compartmentalization, sociologist William J. Goode remarks that there "seems to be no overall set of societal values which explicitly requires consistency or integration from the individual."[1] While this statement points to an important truth, compartmentalization is not merely chaos or lack of integration. The person who depends on compartmentalization as a way of resolving role conflicts may display several very well integrated selves in his everyday life rather than one confused mass of behavior. The businessman-community leader-family man-pillar of the church is not the only person who engages in compartmentalization. Everyone in contemporary complex societies uses this process to some degree. There are many striking examples. One example to balance off the middle-aged and middle-class American male of Main Street is the college student who competitively strives for grades in his courses, seeks relationships of love and sensory stimulation with his friends, and carries on bitter conflicts with his parents.

Frequently compartmentalization does not create serious problems for the individual. If his business, community, family, and religious activities are separated in space and time, the person may not have great trouble in showing a different self in each area of existence. However, when there is an overlap of activities in space and time and the obligations clash in specific situations, compartmentalization is less likely to be a satisfactory strategy. In cases where a person is faced with a challenge to his interpretation of role obligations, he need not compromise or choose one obligation over the other. He has the choice of redefining the conflict through rationalization, providing possible but false reasons for conflict.

In *rationalizing* his behavior, a person tries to show that his actions are consistent with doing his duties. For example, the businessman may rationalize his competitive behavior when he is faced with evidence that it keeps him from being a good Christian by stating that he is the helpless pawn of a system when he is at the office. He may say that his behavior in the firm is determined automatically by the fact that he would lose his job unless he showed competitive behavior. If he is asked why he does not leave business and follow some other occupation he will perhaps state that he has the duty to provide as best he can for his family, that he gives much of what he earns to worthwhile community projects, that he is not as viciously competitive as other businessmen and, most important, if he was not filling the position someone else would be there. Even if each one of these statements were correct, the person would still be rationalizing, because there would still be incompatibility between the duties of economic man and Christian. The fact that he feels a duty to provide a good life for his family, that he is charitable, or that he is not as competitive as other businessmen does not alter the fact that he makes false claims to consumers about his product. The two most widespread rationalizations involve denying responsibility because someone

NOWHERE MAN CHALLENGED (RATIONALIZATION)

would be doing the job in any case or because one was following the orders of a superior. In both of these cases, the person avoids the role conflict by pretending that it does not exist. Also, in both these cases one is denying that he is more than a robot. He implies that at work he is no more than a replaceable part following someone else's program.

COMPROMISE

After compartmentalization, rationalization, and other similar ways of avoiding role conflict, the most common way of achieving role integration is to compromise obligations. While compartmentalization and rationalization are the most important mechanisms for coping with conflict between roles, *compromise* is the key mechanism for coping with conflict within roles. Many significant roles are defined with built in tensions. For example, the role of father in contemporary middle-class America contains serious conflicts. One obligation of the father is to make sure that his children meet certain standards in their behavior. He is supposed to help socialize them into the role of human being that is most common in his community and he must discipline them if they fail to perform this role satisfactorily. He is also expected to equip them to be successful in the future. This means that he is not supposed to allow them to be lazy. He must make sure that they perform as well as they can in school, that they stay out of trouble with the police, and that they have the personalities necessary for making a lasting marriage. All of these responsibilities tend to make the father a figure of respect and discipline. However, the American father is also supposed to be liked by his children. This is not always a problem with the European father, who is often content to gain respect from his children. The American father is expected to be a companion to his children, to play games with them, to listen to their opinions, and to lend a sympathetic ear to their problems. He is supposed to understand why they sometimes fail to measure up to standards and is expected to gain their affection. Although there is no logical contradiction between winning the respect of one's children and gaining their affection, in specific situations it is often impossible to have both at the same time.

NOWHERE MAN CONFUSED (COMPROMISE)

The most frequent resolution of this conflict within the role of father is for the person to strike a compromise between the two requirements. He makes a blend between stern discipline and friendly companionship, usually stressing one or the other. In terms of human relations, he falls somewhere between the pure roles of instrumental leader and affective leader. He marks off certain cases, perhaps those involving drug abuse, crimes against persons and property, and failure in school, as instances in which friendliness must be replaced by discipline. He sets off other cases, such as forgetfulness in performing chores, as instances in which he will not be stern. Through this process of blending the two obligations he creates a personalized role of father which suits his situation.

Willingness to compromise is an important part of the role of human being in the United States. Thus, it is perhaps a more important way of resolving role conflicts in America than it is elsewhere. People are frequently satisfied if they can reach an agreement between conflicting requirements and strike what they consider to be a balance. Many students will be satisfied if they succeed in combining a presentable grade point average with ordinary pleasures and the exploration of new experiences. There are many cases of compromise. However, the person will not always accept a compromise as a satisfactory solution to role conflict. Sometimes he will find it necessary to make a hard choice among competing duties.

CHOICE AMONG COMPETING CLAIMS

Once an expectation has become part of the social self it is relatively difficult to displace it. This is why compartmentalization, rationalization, and compromise are the methods that people usually employ when they are faced with role conflict. However, there are times in every person's life where a clear

NOWHERE MAN BECOMES SOMEBODY
(CHOICE)

WE MUST FIGHT POLLUTION EVEN IF PROFITS ARE LOWER!

choice among competing duties is made. During the twentieth century these cases have been emphasized by existentialist philosophers and other writers. For example, a striking case of choice among roles is that of the civil servant who must decide between following the orders of a superior and committing a crime against humanity. The role of civil servant within a bureaucracy includes the duty to follow the commands of legally positioned authorities in their areas of ability. While a superior may not have the authority to order a civil servant to use window shades rather than venetian blinds in his home, he may have the authority to order him to spy on clients or to lie to them. In some cases he may have the authority to order him to kill others. In the twentieth century a role of human being has slowly become defined which places a responsibility on civil servants to determine whether or not they have been ordered to commit a crime against humanity. This role gives them the duty to avoid carrying out commands involving such crimes. There is no compromise in this case and the person who accepts the role of civil servant and the new role of human being must make a hard choice. As the twentieth century goes on there are more and more calls for making decisive choices rather than compromising. The appeals of ecology and pacifist and civil rights movements are illustrations of such demands. These movements are evidence that compromise is perhaps becoming a less important part of the role of human being in America than it was previously.

SUMMARY

In our present-day world role conflicts are widespread, particularly in the areas where specialization and cultural meetings have gone the farthest. There are three major types of role conflict. First, there is conflict within roles, as when a father experiences tension between his duties to be a disciplinarian and a companion. Second, there is conflict between roles, as when a person experiences tension between his role as a student and his role as a member of a fraternity. Third, there is conflict between two definitions of the same role, as when a clergyman experiences tension between a role requiring him to fight for social change and a role requiring him to minister to the spiritual needs of individuals within his congregation. Role conflict can stem from contradictory duties, as when a person is expected both to do something and not to do the same thing, or from psychologically clashing duties, as when a person feels that he cannot do two duties harmoniously. Role conflict can stem from incompatible obligations, which cannot both be fulfilled in the same situation, or from contradictory obligations, which are experienced by the person as clashing.

There are three major ways of resolving role conflict. First, the person can ignore the conflict by compartmentalizing his activity or rationalizing it. Second, the person can compromise between clashing requirements. Third, the person can choose one obligation over the others. A fourth possibility, creating a new role, while not usually attained, is one of the peak experiences of human life. Man as role maker will be discussed in the next chapter.

Note

[1] William J. Goode, "A Theory of Role Strain," in Edward E. Sampson (ed.), *Approaches, Contexts, and Problems of Social Psychology* (Englewood Cliffs: Prentice-Hall, Inc., 1964), p. 442.

Suggested Readings

Adorno, T. W. *et al., The Authoritarian Personality*, New York: W. W. Norton & Company, Inc., 1969 (paper).

Brown, N. O. *Life Against Death: The Psychoanalytic Meaning of History*, New York: Random House, Inc., 1959 (paper).

Erikson, E. H. *Childhood and Society*, revised edition, New York: W. W. Norton & Company, Inc., 1964 (paper).

Festinger, L. *et al., When Prophecy Fails: A Social and Psychological Study of a Modern Group that Predicted the Destruction of the World*, New York: Harper & Row, Publishers, 1964 (paper).

Freud, S. *Civilization and its Discontents*, W. W. Norton & Company, Inc., 1962 (paper).

Hayakawa, S. I. *et al., Language in Thought and Action*, second edition, New York: Harcourt Brace Jovanovich, Inc., 1963 (paper).

Hoffer, E. *The True Believer*, New York: Harper & Row, Publishers, 1951 (paper).

McClelland, D. C. *The Achieving Society*, New York: D. Van Nostrand Company, Inc., 1961.

Putney, G. and Putney, S. *The Adjusted American: Normal Neuroses in the Individual and Society*, New York: Harper & Row, Publishers, 1964 (paper).

Riesman, D. *et al., The Lonely Crowd: A Study of the Changing American Character*, New Haven: Yale University Press, 1961 (paper).

CHAPTER ELEVEN: HUMAN EXISTENCE AND SOCIAL SELF

Twentieth century thought about human existence has been a dialogue between the social self ("me") and the creative self ("I"). From the perspective of the social self, the human being is a role player, a role taker, and someone who can imagine playing a role. As role player, the person performs tasks according to rights and duties that have been culturally defined or according to expectations that have been defined in social relations. A secretary understands her job description and usually conforms to the expectations of the people at her place of work. As role taker, the person adopts the views of others by asking such questions as, "What would people do and think if I performed this action?" The secretary may take the reactions of her boss into account before she decides to take an extended coffee break.

By role taking, the person learns to expand his existence beyond the immediate present in several ways. First, the person learns how the roles that he is performing fit into much larger tasks including many other roles. The doctor who takes the role of the patient learns that he is involved in a process of healing, going far beyond the simple application of technology to biological matter. The librarian who takes the role of the patron learns that he is involved in a process of education, going beyond the activities of keeping books in place and making sure that they have proper file cards. Second, the person learns to judge his own definitions of roles against the definitions of others. By taking the role of the other he learns how others judge his rights and duties and what others expect of him. The doctor may believe that his duty is to cure disease and his rights include performing any action necessary to securing this end. By taking the roles of patient, hospital administrator, and nurse, he may learn that others see his duties as treating patients with kindness, economizing on medical supplies, and performing only those treatments not assigned to nurses. The doctor will find that if he wants cooperation from others in performing his medical role he will have to adjust to the expectations of significant others. Patients can resist treatments, hospital administrators can be slow to supply space and equipment, and nurses can stick strictly to the rule book in doing their duties. Through role taking the person learns about himself and learns about his range of action with respect to others.

As someone who imagines himself playing a wide variety of roles, the person expands his horizons in other ways. Through the mass media, conversation, and observation the person collects information about roles that he neither plays nor takes directly in specific social relations. This information includes descriptions of roles in other cultures; descriptions of roles within the same culture that are highly specialized; and choices of role definitions offered by social philosophers, commentators and critics. The person may use this information to imagine what his existence would be like if he followed different role definitions. Such ability to imagine expands the person's existence beyond the immediate present and beyond the web of social relations in which he is involved. For example, in playing a role a doctor accepts a set of rights and duties and acts in agreement with them. He may not understand the results of his actions for other people, such as patients, administrators, and nurses, but he follows generally accepted procedures as he has learned them. In taking the roles of others, the doctor learns how his role fits in with the more general task of healing, and what others involved in the task of healing expect of him. However, in imagining himself playing choices of roles of doctor, he learns about possibilities for future action going beyond present specific relations. He may imagine what it would be like if there were no hospitals and doctors practiced in community clinics administered by the people living in neighborhoods. He may imagine what it would be like if doctors were paid a guaranteed annual income by the state and were assigned cases by a board of administrators. Whether or not the doctor believes that these possibilities should be realized in real life, his ability to imagine them makes his future more open and his existence more free.

Learning how to play the cultural definitions of roles gives the person a link with the past. As role player the person is the representative of a cultural tradition. By using his rights and doing his duties, the person gains a claim on some of the resources in the community so that he can satisfy his basic physiological (biological) needs. In return for work people receive income. The person is given resources in exchange for doing a job defined in the past and handed on through tradition. The role of doctor was defined before the young doctor received his M.D. This means that as role player the person becomes civilized. As role taker the person learns how the roles played by him fit into larger tasks, how his actions affect the plans of others, and what others expect of him. Thus, learning how to take roles gives the person links in the present. The doctor learns how his profession fits into the larger task of healing. The focus here is not on the person as representative of a cultural tradition, but on the person as member of a web of social relations. By taking the expectations of others into account, the person gains the respect of others and gains a claim to some of their attention in his search for satisfying wants. By letting the nurse do her job, the doctor insures that the nurse will cooperate with him. He has given others consideration, so they will give him consideration in return. This means that the person has become a social being as well as a civilized being. The role taker is the socially conscious person.

In imagining different role definitions, the person gains a link with the future. The future is not merely a repetition of the past nor a duplication of the present, but a new pattern of existence. It grows out of the links that people have made with the past and that they have made with each other in the present, but it also stems from their plans. By imagining a system of community clinics and acting to attain that dream, the doctor helps create a new future. The focus here is neither on the person as representative of a cultural tradition, nor on the person as member of a web of social relations, but on the person as responsible creator of the future. By taking the future into account through imagining different role definitions, the person becomes a bearer of possibility and gains a claim to some of the resources necessary to experiment with these possibilities. This means that the person has become a creative being as well as a civilized and socially conscious person. One who imagines different futures and different role definitions has at least a measure of creative freedom. He is a man of the future, not only of the past and present.

THE ENTIRE SELF INCLUDES PAST, PRESENT, AND FUTURE

PAST	PRESENT	FUTURE
ROLE DEFINITIONS	RELATIONS WITH OTHERS	NEW POSSIBILITIES
(ROLE OF DOCTOR)	(DOCTOR'S RELATIONS WITH NURSES & PATIENTS)	(THE DREAM OF A NEW CLINIC)

The abilities of the human being do not end with the processes of role playing, role taking, and imagining different role definitions. Each of these three processes is involved closely with the social self ("me"). In playing roles the person acts out what he has learned. The doctor takes a position on a hospital staff and treats patients. In taking roles the person adjusts his actions to the expectations of others. The doctor cooperates with nurses and administrators. In imagining different role definitions the person experiences symbolically choices thought of by others. The doctor imagines a new system of community clinics. However, the person is an individual self ("I") as well as a source of new role definitions. The doctor who imagines himself working in a clinic run by the members of a local community usually gained his ideas from someone else. Perhaps that other person was part of a long line of human beings who passed on the ideas from the individual who first thought of them.

While it is true that over a succession of transmissions any original idea is changed, there is always an individual center of creation. This does not mean that new role definitions come entirely from nowhere. The first person who thought of giving medicine through clinics controlled by communities was probably influenced by previous writings, speeches, and conversations about basing necessary services in communities. He may even have gotten his ideas through observation. For example, he may have noticed that in many communities primary and secondary schools are controlled closely by elected school boards. He may have wondered why hospitals are not similarly controlled by elected medical boards. This, in turn, may have started him thinking about the general problem of local control, and through a long series of steps he may have arrived at the idea of locally controlled and run clinics. All along the way, he would have experienced a lively interplay between social self and individual self.

The creator goes beyond culture and society only by learning to play his own roles well, by learning to take the roles of many others, and by imagining a wide variety of different role definitions already suggested. Only after the social self has developed into maturity is the person ready for a creative leap into the unknown. Those who claim originality without developing their social selves usually unknowingly repeat creations of the past.

ROLE DISTANCE

How can a person take the roles of others, imagine himself playing other roles, and create new role definitions? This question can be answered by considering the implications of the idea that the human self is an ongoing conversation. The individual self ("I") begins discussion by putting forward a plan of action and the social self ("me") looks at that plan and criticizes it in connection with the standards that compose it. The result is submitted to the individual self and a new plan is presented. For example, the "I" may suggest dropping out of college and becoming a beachcomber. The "me" may respond by pointing out that parents, friends, and potential employers would disapprove. The outcome might be a semester's experiment in beachcombing. Entering into this process is action, in which some plans are successful and others are defeated. As a consequence of this action new proposals are made and old ones are given up. The social self changes and includes some new standards. This double process of conversation within the self and of thought and action mutually influencing one another goes on as long as the human being exists. This process holds the key to the explanation of how the human being creates as well as performs roles.

If there is to be a conversation within the self, part of the self must be separate from social and cultural definitions of role. If there is to be thinking about action and thought leading action, part of the self must be separate from action at any particular time. The double separation of part of the self from cultural and social role definitions and from present action is known as *role distance.* The human being always keeps some distance from duties, expectations, and activities. The self that is fully determined by learned roles and present relations is a logical limit never reached in real life.

The experience of role distance is a matter of identification and identity. At some time, every person asks, "Who am I?" The answers to this question make up the *identifications* of the person, and to the extent that these identifications are related to one another in a meaningful pattern they form an *identity*. The identifications made by people are primarily role definitions. These roles can be both general and particular. When one identifies with general roles he answers the question "Who am I?" with such statements as "a man, a human being, a factory worker, a son, a student, a telephone repair man, a brain surgeon at a large urban hospital attached to a university." The sum of the general roles with which a person identifies is the *cultural identity* of that person. When one identifies with particular roles he answers the question, "Who am I?" with such statements as "the son of Mr. and Mrs. Brown, a brain surgeon at the Columbia Presbyterian Medical Center in New York City, a member of a particular social fraternity." The sum of the particular roles with which a person identifies is the *social identity* of that person. The general roles of a person follow from the question, "What would someone in this social position do if I performed this action?" The particular roles of a person follow from the question, "What would some particular other do if I performed this action?" The degree of identification with general and particular roles varies from person to person. Nobody, however, lacks identification with some roles.

The degree to which a person has an identity varies according to how well that person has incorporated his various roles. A person who has organized his other roles around his primary economic role may call himself a doctor, a shoemaker, or a property owner. Karl Marx believed that at the heart of identity were the economic roles performed by people.

A person who has organized his other roles around his primary political role may call himself a citizen, a revolutionary, a conservative, or a liberal. Many thinkers of the New Left hold that a person's political roles are central to his identity. They hold that most problems of the individual are related to the structure of roles within his culture and relations, and that wider participation of people in the decisions affecting them will lead to more understandable identities.

A person who has organized his other roles around his educational roles may call himself an illiterate, a television watcher, a talkative person, or a student. Marshall McLuhan, who has studied the media of communication, believes that educational roles are central in determining identity.

A person who has organized his other roles around his primary appreciative roles may call himself a Christian, a Jew, a son, a mother, a husband, a black, an American, a Chicagoan, or a Southerner. Here, identification is with one's religious, familial, or community roles, rather than with one's economic, political, or educational roles. Of course, the roles involved with all four processes are among every person's identifications. For most people, however, some roles are more important in organizing identity than others, and a group of social psychologists, the symbolic interactionists, has advanced the study of identity by asking people to list answers to the question, "Who am I?"[1] How understandable the answers are will depend, in part, upon the success which the person has met in trying to combine his roles by the various means discussed in the preceding chapter.

While the problems of identification and identity are of great importance to people in the twentieth century, few people are fully identified with their roles. Most people refuse to commit themselves fully to any one or any assortment of their roles. Nobody is simply a student and nothing else. Often while they are playing a role people are aware that part of themselves stands outside of the performance, watching, reserving judgment, and protecting a reserve of the self.

There are three important ways in which people maintain distance from their roles. First, they may remember the fact that it is always possible for them to reject any particular role definition. They do not have to go along with the sets of rights and duties assigned to them culturally, or with the expectations of others that they meet in social relations. For the human being, there is always the possibility of saying "No!"

Second, people may not commit themselves fully to playing any particular role. As they do their duties one part of them may be laughing at the situation, sneering at the other contemptuously, or daydreaming about an entirely different situation. At its extreme this kind of role distance involves becoming a "confidence man" who misleads people about his intentions and takes advantage of them. In situations where a person is being used or being put upon by others, about the only way of keeping the self is by withdrawing a large part of oneself from commitment to the relation. While saying "No" definitely involves a total commitment of the self, keeping oneself apart from role performances requires withdrawal of commitment.

Third, people may maintain role distance by creating new roles going beyond those given to them culturally and socially. Such creation confirms that the person is more than merely an empty vessel for receiving cultural and social definitions. The person becomes a bearer of possibilities.

The three ways of maintaining role distance involve control of the social self ("me") by the individual self ("I"). In the first case the individual self rejects the definitions of the social self without necessarily substituting new definitions. The striking example here is the bureaucrat who refuses to follow an order. Such a civil servant has recognized two important principles. First, he has realized that guilt is personal, not collective. If he behaves immorally he is responsible, not the "system," or any group. Second, he has understood that he must combat the "tyranny of the majority." He must stand up against the weight of "public opinion" which may be pressuring him to behave immorally. He realizes he must take a stand.

In the second case of role distance the individual self does not take part fully in performing the role. The striking example here is the worker who is uninvolved with his job and attempts to make it as much a routine as possible.

In the third case the individual self recombines social and cultural material into a new role definition. In each of these three cases, the individual self is usually set free by role conflict. The presence of competing role definitions in culture and social relations helps the person withstand the strain of following a new course. When the person says "No" to one of his obligations he frequently appeals to another role within the culture, perhaps a role of human being, to justify his departure from expectations. While he does not have to make such an appeal, he usually does so. When the person keeps part of himself apart from current social relations he frequently does so to protect what he has previously gained in other social relations. He does not perform current roles fully because he wants to perform other roles in the future or at least to dream about doing other roles. He also may be afraid of risking failure in a relation and thereby of losing self-esteem. When the person creates a new role, he works from past definitions of choices and offers a new definition for general consideration. Thus, the individual self emerges out of the social self and dips back into it when it has done its work.

CURRENT THREATS TO THE SELF

In the twentieth century many people have concluded that the individual self is under serious attack from many sides. The terms *dehumanization, loss of self, depersonalization*, and *absurdity* have been used to describe the consequences of living in contemporary complex societies. Frequently, people have seen the threats arising from the combinations of tools that have been brought together in the twentieth century. These people claim that twentieth-century human beings live in a technological society. Tools such as hydrogen bombs, electronic communications networks, computers, transportation systems, and factories are believed to have their own force, not open to human intervention. Believers in the technological society hold that tools have gotten out of control and that individual people no longer control their own destinies. Other people disagree with the technological society interpretation and see threats to the self arising from a revolution in products. These observers claim that twentieth-century human beings live in an affluent society, or a consumer society. Products such as color television sets, frozen foods, automobiles, and mass entertainments are believed to cause a mass hypnosis, leading people to be calm about the problems in their environments and blocking out the consideration of new possibilities. Believers in the affluent society hold that people have given up their public responsibilities in favor of private consumption. Still other people have seen threats to the self arising neither from tools nor from products, but from symbol systems. These people claim that twentieth-century human beings live in a scientific society. The symbol systems developed in the specialized branches of science are believed to have created a gulf between the people involved and the people uninvolved, the experts and the laymen. Believers in the scientific society hold that the normal individual cannot understand what happens to him in everyday life, because such understanding requires knowing the symbol systems of science. Finally, still other people see threats to the self arising from systems of rules. These people claim that twentieth-century human beings live in an organizational society. The bureaucracies that dominate present-day social organization are believed to have reduced people to robots performing ordered tasks. Believers in the organizational society hold that the individual self is threatened by the social self represented in organizational rules.

Neither the technological society, the affluent society, the scientific society, nor the organizational society is an adequate name for the structure of human existence in the twentieth century. The development of tools, products, symbols, and rules is a single process. If the individual self is under attack in the twentieth century, the threat arises from all four aspects of culture, not just one. The hydrogen bombs and computers are made in bureaucratic organizations by people who understand scientific symbols and use frozen foods and mass entertainments. The fact that all of the social processes penetrate one another means both that no single process can be made responsible for the threat to the individual and that no single process can be excluded from responsibility. People who say that technology is a neutral means for accomplishing ends, that science is knowledge which can be used both for good purposes and for bad, that one does not have to watch television if he does not want to, or that bureaucratic organization is merely a means for carrying out the people's will efficiently, are speaking in bad faith. The technologies of today represent vast investments in space, time, and resources, and have built-in effects on physical and psychological existence.

In part, McLuhan is correct in saying that the medium is the message. The specialization of symbols and the breaking up of knowledge that seem to be inseparable from scientific thought, do create communications gaps and do drive people apart. In part, science has created an alien culture. Whether or not one takes part directly in the consumer society, he cannot avoid the flood of goods and the level of taste created in it. In part, people are doomed to live in a mass culture, in which refinement and voluntary action are lacking. The massive conglomerate organizations of the present day take up more and more of the individual's space and time. Even when hours of work are cut, the vast organizations enter the person's life through entertainment (mammoth television networks), shopping (large chain stores), worship (churches with millions of members), learning (tremendous state university systems), traveling (global airlines), law enforcement (big city police forces), and most everything else. The organizations are not only his instruments, but are his very social environments. In part, people are ordered in vast bureaucratic organizations.

Thus, the human being in the twentieth century is anxious about the effects of technology on his status as an individual, bewildered by the specialized symbol systems of science, diverted by a flood of consumer goods and entertainments, and powerless to make new actions in enormous organizations. Anxiety replaces confidence, bewilderment replaces understanding, entertainment replaces imagination, and sterility replaces creativity. This description is a summary and a combination of the problems revealed in contemporary life by social critics and commentators of the twentieth century. However, the technological, consumer, scientific, and organizational societies represent only the outside area of threats to the individual self. The internal area is just as important.

The internal area of threats to the individual self centers mainly on the relation of the individual self to the social self. There are four ways in which these threats are made apparent. First, there is the fear that the individual self will be fully absorbed by the social self. This is the danger that some human beings will become fully identified with their roles and will, therefore, lose role distance. They will no longer be able to say "No" to organizational commands or to the expectations of people they know. They will believe that organizations are greater than they are and that organizations, not people, are to be praised and blamed.

THE HOUSE THAT JACK BUILT (FINAL VISIT)

1. JACK HAS AN ELECTRIC BUTTER KNIFE (TECHNOLOGICAL SOCIETY)

2. JACK EATS ARTIFICIAL CAVIAR ON A SLICE OF ARTIFICIAL BREAD (AFFLUENT SOCIETY)

3. JACK IS A BIOLOGIST SPECIALIZING IN THE MATING HABITS OF THE YELLOW BELLIED SAP SUCKER (SCIENTIFIC SOCIETY)

4. JACK WORKS FOR ENORMOUS EDUCATIONAL ENTERPRISES, INC. (ORGANIZATIONAL SOCIETY)

Second, there is the feeling that people are becoming increasingly bewildered about what roles to play, particularly the role of human being and other such general, though important, roles. This is the danger that the social self is dissolving and that there is no material with which to make a new combination. Here, the idea is that people will no longer be able to say "No" because they have nothing to believe in, and that they will no longer be able to create because they have nothing to go beyond. The feeling is that without standards people will not be able to stand up to the tyranny of the majority.

Third, there is the belief that people are exposed to so much role conflict that they cannot create identities. This is the danger that the social self is too divided to permit combination. As in the case of bewilderment caused by dissolving the social self, the idea is that people will have nothing of their own to enable them to withstand the burden of obligations and expectations. The feeling is that people will be so torn apart that they will follow shifting public opinion like slaves.

Fourth, there is the belief that the very roles contained in the social self are destructive. This is the danger that the social self is self-defeating because it contains commands to compete and engage in conflict rather than to cooperate and engage in altruism. Here, the idea is that the social self blocks constructive creation by the individual self.

Probably the most widespread fear is that people will become absorbed in their roles and will lose the ability to say "No" to demands made on them. Such absorption occurs when the person takes the social self as the highest guide in all of his action. In the beginning of this book the social self was introduced by considering the meaning of the question, "What would people think if I did this?" The person who is completely involved in his social roles continuously asks this question and acts in such a way that he will receive approval from others. He gives up his own initiative in making decisions for guidance by prevailing standards. He justifies his actions by calling upon an argument familiar to children. Frequently, when a child wants something from his parents and is challenged to give a reason for his having it, he will say, "The other kids have it, so I should have it, too." Similarly, when a child faces punishment for something that he has done and is asked to explain why he has done it, he will say, "The other kids did it, too, so why are you blaming me?"

Children are not the only people who are *inauthentic* in excusing their actions by saying that they are only going along with the crowd. People often make demands and excuse themselves by arguing that they are only going along with generally expected behavior. Sometimes they go so far as to claim that they "had to" perform certain actions because "everyone else" was performing them. When a person uses this kind of rationalization enough he has lost the aspect of distance from his roles which allows him to say "No." The individual self ("I") has become a slave to the social self ("me"), and the only function of the individual self is to ask the question, "What would people think if I did this?"

The problem of the absorption of the individual self into the social self has become critical in the twentieth century because of the vastly increased range and scale of organization and communications. Bureaucratically organized political systems controlling advanced communications networks have on occasion created general expectations of conflict and hatred. In Nazi Germany the ordinary citizen who gave up his individual self to his social self felt justified in helping commit mass murder against other ethnic groups. Losing role distance, he became a criminal against humanity. In parts of the United States, ordinary people who give up their individual selves to their social selves sometimes feel justified in discriminating against people because of their race. The roles contained in the social self vary according to time, place, and culture, and they do not always represent the ideals of the Judaeo-Christian tradition. When they made it a duty to hate others and to harm them, the person who has lost role distance and who has become identified with his roles will strike out against others and will feel justified in doing so. When a person is completely involved in his roles he has lost his status as an individual and has become a relatively advanced robot. Even in a technological, scientific, affluent, and organizational society, however, such surrender is not inevitable.

A second fear that haunts many people in the twentieth century is that the social self is dissolving, and that people are losing their ability to create new roles. In the past, the central roles in social existence have been the roles of human being carried in the religious traditions. During the last 400 years in the West the unity of Roman Catholicism has been broken and the Judaeo-Christian tradition itself has gradually lost its hold on successive generations. No single body of thought has taken the place of the religious tradition in Western life. For some people science supplies an adequate role of human being and for others the role of human being is found in philosophies of history such as Marxism or various cults. Many people are simply not aware that they could take any role of human being. According to those who believe that the social self is dissolving, the lack of any widely held role of human being has created despair, bewilderment, and confusion in Western populations. They argue that people have lost their bearings and drift aimlessly from one situation to the next without rhyme or reason. They claim that when people have no role of human being to take they shift from being passive and disinterested to being violent and emotional. At times they are a mass, like a herd of sheep, and at other times a mob, like a stampede of cattle. Lacking traditional standards of judgment, people are willing to follow demagogic leaders who promise them a way out of confusion.

Like the person who is absorbed, completely involved, in his roles, the bewildered person cannot say "no." However, the bewildered person is also incapable of creating new roles to take him out of his situation. Significant creation can only take place within a tradition. The richer the tradition the better the creation. The role of scientist, for example, was created slowly out of roles performed in some monasteries in the Middle Ages. Similarly, the role of entrepreneur was created out of the role of merchant in the Middle Ages. When tradition dissolves there is no point at which creation can occur. Thus, the individual self needs the social self to become a creator of roles.

Many people in the twentieth century are haunted by a third fear that the social self is hopelessly divided, and that all of the methods of integration discussed in the preceding chapter are incapable of producing even a minimum of agreement. Here, the problem is neither that the individual self may become absorbed, involved, in the social self, nor that the individual self will face an emptiness, but that the social self will become so divided into conflicting parts that the individual self will have nothing to protect in specific situations. Commentators who fear absorption point to the ways in which people in the contemporary world give up their responsibility to judge expectations and obligations. Commentators who fear bewilderment point out that current Western cultural life lacks any unifying themes. But observers who fear division point to the fact that contemporary human existence is divided among many compartments, each one with its specialized characteristics and roles.

In the economic process the person may be an economic man, competing with others and acting to gain the largest amount of goods. In the political process the person may be a political man, in conflict with others to have his plans backed up by the means to organized violence. In the educational process the person may be a learning man, coming to understand the various aspects of his culture. In the appreciative process the person may be a social man, seeking approval from others. So divided into parts, the person works against himself. There is a gap between his understanding of the culture and the acts that he performs in the political and economic processes. In competing for goods he loses approval, and in seeking approval he loses power. He is caught in vicious contradiction.

When the social self is too divided the individual self loses role distance. To maintain the type of role distance defined as keeping oneself apart from role performances, the self must have a center. When the self is divided it has no center, and the person is at the mercy of the demands put in each specific situation. He goes through a succession of selves, and is committed to each one. The descriptions of the divided self and the dissolving self point to different aspects of the same situation. When the social self dissolves it loses any unifying role of human being. The person is left adrift. However, he is not really left adrift in a void. He is left to drift between his various functional roles. Further, the description of the self absorbed in social roles points to yet another aspect of the same situation. Lacking a unifying role of human being and drifting among various functional roles, the person becomes absorbed in the expectations of the moment, continually looking for guidance by asking the question, "What would people think if I did this?" Thus, the self absorbed in social roles, the bewildered self, and the divided self combine in a description of an individual self that has lost role distance from the social self.

FOUR MORE FACES OF NOWHERE MAN

Behind fears of absorption, bewilderment, and division is the fear that by their very content the most important roles in contemporary social existence work to defeat the individual self. Roles in which the person is rewarded for taking advantage of others or for harming them often cancel or even over-balance roles in which the person is rewarded for cooperating with others or helping them. There is no reason that the individual should not flourish best in a set of relations emphasizing exchange, cooperation, and altruism. In each of these three kinds of relation the individual is encouraged to make a contri-bution to gaining some goal. In competition and conflict, however, the indi-vidual uses his energy attempting to get more of some good than someone else or to prevent someone else from reaching goals. Yet despite the advan-tages of exchange, cooperation, and altruism to the development of the indi-vidual self, competition and conflict are frequently stressed in contemporary social existence.

THE ONE FACE OF AUTHENTIC MAN

I CAN HELP CREATE NEW ROLES BY SAYING "NO" TO IMMORAL COMMANDS, JOINING WITH OTHERS IN MAKING NEW STANDARDS, HELPING TO PUT THE DIVIDED SELF TOGETHER AGAIN, STRESSING COOPERATION AND ALTRUISM IN MY ACTIONS.

Rather than sharpening the individual self, competition tends to make everyone the same. All are engaged in the same race and all must learn the same skills to survive and perhaps to triumph. Cooperation, however, does sharpen the individual self, because each person is encouraged to make his own contribution to the common effort. Similarly, conflict tends to make people similar. As they seek to destroy one another, enemies tend to take on the same brutal characteristics. They come to resemble the stereotypes with which they slur one another. Altruism, however, makes the individual self even more distinctive because as it opens itself to the other's experience it gains an even more rich and complex identity. This does not mean that competition and conflict can be easily removed from human existence. There is a scarcity of space, time, and resources for the realization of the various possibilities desired by human beings. This means that some competition is probably unavoidable. However, there is no reason to claim that it is impossible to redesign current social roles so that cooperation and exchange will be rewarded more than competition and conflict. Such a change, combined with a new role of human being constructed out of the world's great cultural traditions, is the best hope for restoring the vigorous dialogue between individual self and social self which is necessary for personal fulfillment and human advancement.

SUMMARY

Human beings exist by playing roles, taking roles, imagining themselves playing roles, and creating new roles. As role player the person performs a task assigned to him in agreement with culturally defined rights and duties and socially defined expectations. As role taker the person expands his horizons by seeing himself from the viewpoints of others and by coming to appreciate the implications of his task for larger projects. As someone who imagines himself playing roles the person expands his horizons even further. He becomes a bearer of possibilities for new kinds of human existence. Finally, as a creator of new roles, the person becomes a direct contributor to civilization and the enrichment of other selves.

To create, the individual self must keep some distance from the social self so that they can engage in a dialogue. There are three major kinds of role distance. First, the individual self may keep some independence from the social self by saying "No" to role duties and expectations. Second, the individual self may hold itself apart from particular role performances. One may laugh at oneself or at the social situation. Third, the individual self may create new roles to go beyond the ones contained in the social self.

Many commentators note significant threats to the individual self in the twentieth century. The individual self is threatened with absorption into social roles, confusion caused by lack of a unifying role of human being, division of the social self into conflicting roles, and obligations or duties to take part in competition and conflict built into roles. These threats combine in a description of the individual self progressively losing distance from the social self. Human advance depends upon restoring a dialogue between "I" and "me."

Note

[1] Jerome G. Manis and Bernard N. Meltzer, *Symbolic Interaction* (Boston: Allyn and Bacon, Inc., 1967).

Suggested Readings

Barrett, W. *What Is Existentialism*, New York: Grove Press, Inc., 1964 (paper).

Camus, A. *The Rebel: An Essay on Man in Revolt*, New York: Random House, Inc., 1954 (paper).

Fromm, E. *The Revolution of Hope*, New York: Bantam Books, 1968 (paper).

Galbraith, J. K. *The Affluent Society*, New York: New American Library of World Literature, Inc., 1969 (paper).

Jaspers, K. *Man in the Modern Age*, Garden City: Doubleday & Company, Inc., 1957 (paper).

Merleau-Ponty, M. *Humanism and Terror*, Boston: The Beacon Press, 1969 (paper).

Mumford, L. *The Pentagon of Power*, New York: Harcourt Brace Jovanovich, Inc., 1970.

Strauss, A. L. *Mirrors and Masks: The Search for Identity*, Glencoe: The Free Press, 1959.

De Chardin, P. T. *The Phenomenon of Man*, New York: Harper & Row, Publishers, 1959 (paper).

GLOSSARY INDEX